One Pan, Two Plates

One Pan, Two Plates

MORE THAN 70 COMPLETE
WEEKNIGHT MEALS FOR TWO

Carla Snyder

PHOTOGRAPHS BY *Jody Horton*

CHRONICLE BOOKS

SAN FRANCISCO

Library of Congress Cataloging-in-Publication
Data available.

ISBN 978-1-4521-0670-0

Manufactured in China

Designed by *Cat Grishaver*
Food and prop styling by *Kate LeSueur*

20 19 18 17 16 15 14 13 12

Chronicle Books LLC
680 Second Street
San Francisco, California 94107
www.chroniclebooks.com

FOR MY KIDS,

Jessica, Justin, and Corey;

AND FOR THE COUNTLESS OTHERS WHO COOK FOR TWO
WITH JOY, EXCITEMENT, AND ANTICIPATION.

contents

a case for cooking

On the trip home from work, our minds are often churning with all the things that need to be done . . . cleaning, laundry, bills, e-mail, and the chore of making dinner. With so little time in the day for all that must be accomplished, it seems unfair to return home to the immediate task of creating a meal. But it isn't so much the actual cooking that's driven most of us to high-fat takeout and pricey restaurants—it's the hour-plus of organizing, shopping, prepping, and cleaning up. Wouldn't it be nice to stay home and produce a delicious, healthful, hot meal in less than 1 hour, with easy prep and minimal cleanup? Maybe even share a glass of wine with your significant other?

I can't help you with your laundry or bills, but *One Pan, Two Plates* can help you get a healthful meal on the table in less time and with less cleanup. All the dishes are complete made-from-scratch meals, with one-pan cleanup and ready to eat in less than 1 hour (many less than 30 minutes). These are not your grandmother's casseroles, but enticing dishes like Skirt Steak Fajitas with Pico de Gallo and Avocado (page 90), Black Cod Fillets Poached in Five-Spice Broth with Baby Bok Choy and Udon (page 181), and Fettuccine with Scallops, Carrots, and Ginger-Lime Butter Sauce (page 24). How is this possible? I plumbed my twenty-five years of knowledge as a cooking school instructor, caterer, and recipe developer to find ways to orchestrate components with similar cooking techniques into complete meals in a single pan.

It's simple, really. Take Sautéed Pork Chops with Sweet Potato, Apple, and Mustard Sauce (page 79). The recipe begins with a simple sauté of two pork chops. The chops are removed from the pan when partially cooked, and thin slices of sweet potato and apple are added to the hot pan along with a sprinkle of cinnamon and a splash of cider. That aromatic mix is covered and cooked until almost tender, and then the pork chops are returned to the pan and the whole thing is finished in a few more minutes, with perfectly tender chops. After you arrange the pork and potato mixture on plates, a quick sauce comes together by simply whisking a tablespoon or so of Dijon mustard into the pan juices. A drizzle of sauce and dinner is done—a fresh, healthful meal that's balanced in flavor and pretty on the plate, all in less than an hour with one pan to clean.

Whether you are a young couple just starting out or empty nesters, you'll find it much cheaper and quicker to cook recipes for two instead of the usual four to six servings you find in main-course recipes. Cooking for two also means that you'll have no surplus food to wrap up, refrigerate, and incorporate into another meal within a few days. Imagine, no more guilty leftovers tossed in the trash because they went bad or they just weren't appealing reheated in the microwave the next day.

With the recipes in this book, you are also spared having to put time and thought into side dishes, since the whole meal has been composed for you. One of the biggest dilemmas for home cooks is what to serve alongside the roast chicken or beef tips. In *One Pan, Two Plates*, the complete meal is right there.

THE CARBOHYDRATE CURE

CHAPTER

1

pastas, grains & hot sandwiches

Three-Cheese Mac

with CRISPY PROSCIUTTO

There is nothing that delivers comfort and a little pampering like creamy, rich macaroni and cheese. I add crispy, fried prosciutto for its salt and hammy flavor, and because dinner is just usually more, well, dinnerlike for my husband if it contains a little meat. This version includes my top three cheeses: goat cheese, Parmesan, and Gruyère. For extra TLC, add a glass of wine, an extra log on the fire, and something chocolate for dessert.

Salt	*1 1/2 cups/360 ml milk,*
2 cups/225 g elbow macaroni	*warmed in the microwave*
4 tbsp/55 g unsalted butter	*1/3 cup/55 g crumbled goat cheese*
6 thin slices prosciutto,	*1/3 cup/40 g freshly grated Parmesan cheese*
cut crosswise into strips	*1/3 cup/40 g shredded Gruyère cheese*
1/2 cup/55 g panko bread crumbs	*Pinch of freshly grated nutmeg*
1 1/2 tbsp all-purpose flour	*Freshly ground black pepper*

1. Preheat the oven to 350°F/180°C/gas 4. Position a rack in the center.

2. Fill a 12-in/30.5-cm ovenproof skillet, preferably cast iron, with water up to about 1 in/2.5 cm from the top. Cover and bring to a boil over high heat. Add 2 tsp salt and toss in the macaroni. Stir gently once or twice so the pasta doesn't stick.

3. Reduce the heat to medium-high. You must cook the macaroni at a gentle boil only until it's still just short of completely tender, because it will finish cooking in the oven. For example, if the box says to cook for 7 minutes, test the pasta after 5 minutes. To check, fish a piece out of the water (a slotted spoon makes it easy), run it under cold water, and bite it. It should still be chewy, but not tough. Drain the pasta in a colander set in the sink and run cold water over it to stop the cooking and keep it from clumping.

continued

4. Add 2 tbsp of the butter to the pan and melt over medium-high heat. Add the prosciutto and toss it around in the pan until it's crispy, about 2 minutes. Transfer the prosciutto to a plate. Put the panko in a small bowl. Pour the hot butter left in the pan over the panko and toss to coat.

5. Return the pan to medium-high heat and add the remaining 2 tbsp butter. When the butter is melted, sprinkle in the flour and 1/4 tsp salt. Cook, stirring, until the flour becomes foamy, about 1 minute. Whisk in the warm milk. Stir until the mixture is thickened and saucy, about 2 minutes. Remove from the heat and add all three cheeses, the nutmeg, and a grind or two of pepper, stirring until the cheeses are melted. Taste and season with more salt and pepper if it needs it. Stir in the macaroni and prosciutto until all of the mac is thoroughly coated and the prosciutto is evenly distributed. Smooth the top and sprinkle the buttery bread crumbs over the top.

6. Transfer to the oven and bake for about 20 minutes, or until the juices are bubbly and the top is lightly browned. If you have time to give it a few more minutes, the top will get even crispier. Scoop into warmed shallow bowls and serve hot.

it's that easy: Macaroni and cheese for two makes a simple yet lovely meal when paired with a green salad, crusty bread, and a glass of wine. I prefer to make and serve it in a cast-iron skillet, because the pan holds the heat so well. One time, I put the skillet on the table, set out two forks, and my husband and I devoured it right out of the pan. It was delicious that way because the cheesy sauce was oozy and hot throughout the whole meal. It was also fun to fight over the larger pieces of prosciutto with our forks . . . a kind of forky swordplay if you will.

extra hungry? Pair this pasta dish with a simple salad if you're craving a bit of green stuff. It doesn't have to be complicated—just a handful of greens, a squirt of fresh lemon juice, and a glug of olive oil should do it.

in the glass: It's tough to find a low-priced white Burgundy, but they are out there if you look. Try to find Vincent Girardin Bourgogne. It's a Chardonnay with lots of crisp apple to counteract the richness of the cheese, but it's still light and is made without the profuse heavy oak that makes so many Chardonnays tough to pair with food.

Fresh Summer Pasta

with TOMATOES, GARLIC, BASIL, *and* BUTTERY CROUTONS

Fresh tomatoes, fresh basil, garlic, and pasta could be dinner every night at my house. Since you use fresh tomatoes, this dish should be reserved for that time of year when they are perfectly ripe and at peak flavor. It might seem like carb overload, but the crispy croutons add an addictive buttery crunch, so don't even think about leaving them out. The amount of garlic, red pepper flakes, and basil is a personal thing, so be sure to tailor this dish to your taste buds.

1 large tomato, cored and diced (see "It's that easy")

2 garlic cloves, minced

2 ¹/₂ tsp salt

2 tbsp extra-virgin olive oil

2 tsp balsamic vinegar

¹/₄ tsp red pepper flakes

Freshly ground black pepper

2 tbsp unsalted butter

3 thick slices Italian-style bread, cut into 1-in/2.5-cm cubes (see "It's that easy")

10 oz/250 g fresh fettuccine

¹/₃ cup/10 g thinly sliced fresh basil leaves

1. In a large bowl big enough to hold the pasta later, combine the tomato, half of the garlic, ¹/₄ tsp of the salt, the olive oil, vinegar, red pepper flakes, and a few grinds of black pepper and toss it all together. Set aside.

2. In a 12-in/30.5-cm skillet over medium heat, melt the butter. Add the bread cubes, the remaining garlic, and ¹/₄ tsp salt and cook until the bread cubes are browned in the hot fat, turning them as they crisp, about 5 minutes total. They will soak up all the butter in the pan like sponges. (You may need to reduce the heat if they threaten to over-brown.) Transfer the croutons to a plate. Let the pan cool slightly before carefully wiping it out with paper towels.

3. Fill the skillet with water up to about 1 in/2.5 cm from the top. Cover and bring to a boil over high heat. Add the remaining 2 tsp salt and the

continued

fettuccine. Stir gently once or twice so the noodles don't stick. Cook, stirring occasionally, until al dente, about 3 minutes or according to the package directions. (To check, fish out a strand and bite into it. It should still be chewy, but not tough.) Scoop out about 1/4 cup/60 ml of the pasta-cooking water and set it aside, then drain the pasta in a colander set in the sink.

4. Immediately dump the pasta and 1 to 2 tbsp of the reserved pasta water into the bowl with the tomato mixture and toss to coat the pasta thoroughly. Add the basil and croutons and stir to incorporate them into the mix. Taste and adjust the seasoning. If it seems dry, add a little more pasta water.

5. Heap the pasta on warmed plates and eat with reckless abandon. The pasta cools really quickly and the croutons get soggy, so tuck in right away.

it's that easy: Tomato skins can be incredibly tough! The easiest way to slice them is to use a serrated knife. After your first cuts, lay the tomato slices flat with any skin sides down; you shouldn't have any trouble cutting them into cubes. The same thing goes for crusty artisan loaves of bread. Use a serrated knife to saw through the crispy crust and tender insides.

extra hungry? A small salad of arugula with grated or shaved Parmesan will go nicely with all the basil in the pasta. You could toss in a few olives if you have them.

in the glass: If you haven't tried one lately, this dish is a great excuse to drink a dry, crisp rosé. The Coppola winery makes wine with a good price-to-quality ratio, and it is widely distributed, thus easy to find. Look for Francis Ford Coppola Winery Sofia Rosé. It has a crisp acidity but with enough fruit to complement the tomatoes, and enough spice to stand up to the garlic.

Fettuccine

with SCALLOPS, CARROTS, *and* GINGER-LIME BUTTER SAUCE

Fettuccine has such a wonderful chewy texture, especially when the pasta is fresh. Lucky for us, fresh pasta is easy to find these days in the refrigerated and frozen foods section of most well-stocked groceries and almost any Italian-foods store. I love to pair it with silky things like butter and scallops and, as in this dish, a touch of lime. The citrus and the spice of fresh ginger wake up the buttery carrots and embellish the noodles like a colorful scarf on a simple black dress. Speaking of simple, this dish is pretty basic. Once the carrots are cut, you're just a few steps away from having dinner on the table in minutes flat.

Salt	*Freshly ground black pepper*
10 oz/280 g fresh fettuccine	*2 garlic cloves, minced*
4 tbsp/55 g unsalted butter	*12 oz/340 g day-boat*
1 shallot, minced	*(also called dry or dry-packed; see Note)*
	scallops, patted dry on paper towels
1 tbsp peeled and minced fresh ginger	
2 large carrots, peeled and cut into matchsticks (see "It's that easy")	*1 lime, ½ reserved for juice, ½ cut into wedges for garnish*
	1 tbsp minced fresh chives

1. Fill a 12-in/30.5-cm skillet with water up to about 1 in/2.5 cm from the top. Cover and bring to a boil over high heat. Add 2 tsp salt and toss in the fettuccine. Stir gently once or twice so the noodles don't stick. Cook, stirring occasionally, until al dente, about 3 minutes or according to the package directions. (To check, fish out a strand and bite into it. It should still be chewy, but not tough.) Scoop out ½ cup/120 ml of the pasta-cooking water and set it aside. Drain the pasta in a colander set in the sink and run just enough cold water over it to stop the cooking but leave it warm.

2. In the same pan, melt 2 tbsp of the butter over medium-high heat. Add the shallot, ginger, and carrots. Sprinkle with salt and pepper and sauté the vegetables until they are crisp-tender and lightly browned, about 4 minutes. Add the garlic and sauté for another minute. Scoop the vegetables out of the pan onto a warmed plate (or cover the plate loosely with aluminum foil to keep warm).

3. Sprinkle the scallops with salt and pepper on both sides. Return the pan to medium-high heat and add the remaining 2 tbsp butter. When it's melted and sizzling, add the scallops. Cook until browned on the first side, about 2 minutes (don't try to move them sooner or they will stick and tear). Using tongs or a spatula, carefully turn them over and sear on the second side for another 2 minutes. They should be browned and slightly firm to the touch when pressed with a finger. Transfer the scallops to another warmed plate and cover to keep them warm.

4. Still over medium-high heat, add half of the reserved pasta-cooking water to the hot pan and squeeze in the juice from the lime half. Add the pasta and toss for about 1 minute to heat it and coat it with the sauce. Add the vegetables and toss them with the pasta to warm them up. Taste for seasoning and add more salt and pepper, if desired. If the mixture seems dry, stir in a little more of the reserved pasta water.

5. Mound the pasta onto warmed plates and top it with the scallops, dividing them evenly. Sprinkle with the chives, garnish the plates with the lime wedges, and serve hot.

note: *Seek out day-boat scallops, which are fresher and not chemically treated.*

it's that easy: *To cut a carrot into matchsticks, peel it first and trim off the pointy and stem ends. Cut crosswise into pieces about 4 in/10 cm long. Cut a very thin slice from one long side of a piece so the carrot will sit on the cutting board without rolling. Cut downward, lengthwise, into 1/8-in/3-mm slices. Stack the slices flat-side up and cut the stack lengthwise into 1/8-in/3-mm sticks. Cut the sticks in half so that they are about 2 in/5 cm long, like matchsticks. Voilà!*

extra hungry? *A beautiful, ripe sliced tomato dressed with salt, pepper, and a splash of extra-virgin olive oil would be perfect alongside this rich dish.*

in the glass: *Whites rule as an accompaniment to this scallop dish; a California Sauvignon Blanc from Edna Valley would reign supreme.*

Linguine

with CHICKEN, SPINACH, *and* FETA CHEESE

I had a friend in college who would wiggle in her chair whenever she was eating something really delicious. As an eater and a cook, I really appreciate that kind of enthusiasm at the table. I know Lynn would really love this pasta dish because it's delicious, quick, and easy to pull together for a busy weeknight meal. She'd love the tender chicken, chewy pasta, salty cheese, and fresh spinach, which is irresistible by the way. Last but not least, the lemon in this dish is so bright with tart fruit; I know that it would make her smile . . . and wiggle a little bit in her chair.

Salt	*Freshly ground black pepper*
10 oz/280 g fresh linguine	*One 5-oz/140-g bag baby spinach*
2 tbsp olive oil	*1 cup/115 g crumbled feta cheese*
1 small onion, thinly sliced	*1/3 cup/75 ml lemon juice, plus more if needed*
2 boneless skinless chicken breasts, diced	*Red pepper flakes (optional)*

1. Fill a 12-in/30.5-cm skillet with water up to about 1 in/2.5 cm from the top. Cover and bring to a boil over high heat. Add 2 tsp salt and toss in the linguine. Stir gently once or twice so the noodles don't stick. Cook, stirring occasionally, until al dente, about 3 minutes or according to the package directions. (To check, fish out a strand and bite into it. It should still be chewy, but not tough.) Scoop out 1/2 cup/120 ml of the pasta-cooking water and set it aside. Drain the pasta in a colander set in the sink and run just enough cold water over it to stop the cooking but leave it warm.

2. Reduce the heat to medium-high and add the olive oil to the hot pan along with the onion and cook until the onion softens a little, about 2 minutes. Add the chicken, 1/2 tsp salt, and a sprinkling of pepper and sauté the chicken until it is almost cooked, about 2 minutes. Add a little of the reserved pasta water to clean up any brown bits on the bottom of the pan. Add the spinach to the pan by the handful and cook, stirring and tossing until it has wilted. Return the drained pasta to the pan and add the feta cheese and lemon juice. Toss the mixture until the cheese has melted a little and season again with more salt and pepper if it needs it. You might want to add more lemon juice or pasta water as well. It's up to you. If you like a little heat, a pinch of red pepper flakes is a welcome addition.

3. Mound the pasta onto two heated plates and serve hot.

it's that easy: This dish is easy for me to pull together because I always have the ingredients on hand: boneless skinless chicken breasts and fresh pasta in the freezer; lemons, feta, and spinach in the fridge; and onions in the pantry. It's so easy. It really is.

extra hungry? Add a little green salad of butter lettuce, radicchio, and orange tossed with a glug of olive oil, salt, and lots of pepper.

in the glass: A Beaujolais from Jadot would be my choice with this dish but if you're looking for white you can't go wrong with a bottle of Kim Crawford Sauvignon Blanc.

Fresh Pepper Linguine

with OLIVE OIL–PACKED TUNA, CAPERS, *and* GOLDEN RAISINS

You gotta love a dinner that is sourced almost entirely from the pantry. It sits in the cupboard, just waiting to sustain you on dark, hungry nights. And it's good . . . so good. Fresh black-pepper linguine with salty capers, sweet golden raisins, zesty orange, grassy fresh parsley, and a can of olive oil–packed tuna all tossed together with a garlicky dressing comes together in about 20 minutes to make a weeknight dinner that's delicious, simple, and fast.

1 orange	*One 5-oz/140-g can*
Salt	*olive oil–packed tuna, drained*
10 oz/280 g fresh black-pepper linguine	*¼ cup/40 g golden raisins*
(see "It's that easy")	*2 tbsp capers, rinsed*
¼ cup/60 ml extra-virgin olive oil	*4 tbsp/5 g minced fresh flat-leaf parsley*
1 small yellow onion, diced	*Freshly ground black pepper*
2 garlic cloves, minced	

1. Fill a 12-in/30.5-cm skillet with water up to about 1 in/2.5 cm from the top. Cover and bring to a boil over high heat.

2. While the water is heating, use a Microplane or the small holes on a box grater to remove the zest from the orange. Set the zest aside. Switch to a knife and remove the rest of the peel and bitter white pith from the orange. Discard the peel and cut the flesh into bite-size sections. Set the flesh aside with the zest.

3. Add 2 tsp salt to the boiling water and toss in the linguine. Stir gently once or twice so the noodles don't stick. Cook, stirring occasionally, until al dente, about 3 minutes or according to the package directions. (To check, fish out a strand and bite into it. It should still be chewy, but not tough.) Scoop out about ¼ cup/60 ml of the pasta-cooking water and set it aside. Drain the pasta in a colander set in the sink and run just enough cold water over it to stop the cooking but not completely cool it off.

4. Quickly place the hot pan over medium-high heat and add the olive oil. When the oil is so hot it shimmers (but is not smoking), add the onion and garlic and cook, stirring constantly, until the onion begins to soften and the garlic is fragrant, about 1 minute. Add the tuna, orange zest and flesh, raisins, and capers and toss the sauce for another minute or so to warm it through. Return the pasta to the pan along with about half of the reserved pasta-cooking water and half of the parsley, tossing with tongs to reheat the pasta and coat it nicely with the sauce. Taste and add more salt, a grind or two of pepper, and/or a little more of the pasta water to flavor and moisten as desired.

5. Pile the pasta onto warmed plates, garnish with the remaining parsley, and serve hot.

it's that easy: I direct you to use fresh pasta for a few reasons: 1) I think it tastes best; 2) it has a nice chewy texture; 3) it cooks fast. My market sells a local company's fresh pasta products, but there are nationally distributed brands as well. Try a few until you find the brands that suit you. It's a tough job, but someone has to do it.

extra hungry? Dice a big, ripe tomato and toss it with 1 teaspoon minced garlic, a splash of balsamic vinegar, and a drizzle of olive oil. Mound it onto crispy bread rounds and top it with a little grated Parmesan or feta cheese. It's like a little appetizer with your meal.

in the glass: A crispy, fruity rosé is delicious with this pasta dish. Stick with the Italian theme and go for something Sicilian like Tasca d'Almerita Regaleali Rose.

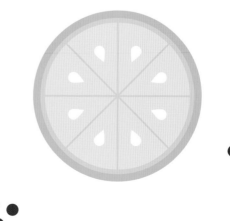

Pasta Carbonara

Classic pasta carbonara is rich, smoky, salty, and cheesy—the epitome of comfort food. What makes this dish a classic is the egg-centric sauce that thickens just enough when tossed with the hot pasta, crispy bacon, and nutty Parmesan. Though pasta carbonara isn't exactly health food, I believe that everyone could use a heaping helping of carbohydrate comfort on a regular basis. You can decide whether you need it monthly, weekly, or daily. I'm not here to judge!

2 1/4 tsp salt

10 oz/280 g fresh linguine

2 large eggs, beaten

Freshly ground black pepper

1 tbsp olive oil

4 slices bacon, chopped

2 garlic cloves, minced

1/2 cup/55 g freshly grated Parmesan or Pecorino Romano cheese (see "It's that easy")

2 tsp minced fresh flat-leaf parsley

1. Fill a 12-in/30.5-cm skillet with water up to about 1 in/2.5 cm from the top. Cover and bring to a boil over high heat. Add 2 tsp of the salt and toss in the linguine. Stir gently once or twice so the noodles don't stick.

2. Meanwhile, in a bowl, whisk together the eggs, remaining 1/4 tsp salt, and a few grinds of pepper. Set aside.

3. Cook the pasta for about 2 minutes, or 1 minute less than directed on the package. It's important that the pasta isn't completely cooked at this point. (To check, fish out a strand and bite into it. It should still be chewy, but not tough.) Don't worry, the pasta will finish cooking in the sauce. Scoop out about 1/4 cup/60 ml of the pasta-cooking water and whisk about 2 tbsp into the egg mixture. Set the rest of the pasta water aside. Drain the pasta in a colander set in the sink and run just enough cold water over it to stop the cooking. It should still be hot.

4. Put the empty skillet over medium-high heat and add the olive oil and chopped bacon. Cook the bacon, stirring often, until crispy, about 3 minutes. Using a slotted spoon, transfer the bacon to the egg mixture and remove the pan from the heat.

5. Add the garlic to the pan and cook it in the hot bacon fat, off the heat, until fragrant, about 20 seconds. It should sizzle. Return the drained pasta to the pan and toss it in the hot bacon fat for about 1 minute to reheat it. Quickly pour in the egg mixture and all but about 2 tbsp of the cheese and toss to blend the ingredients thoroughly. The egg mixture should thicken into a sauce. Add more of the reserved pasta water if it seems dry. Taste and adjust the seasoning.

6. Heap the pasta onto warmed plates. Garnish with the reserved cheese and the parsley and serve hot.

variation: This classic recipe of pasta, eggs, smoked pork, and cheese is extremely versatile, so once you've mastered this dish, go ahead and get creative. Try adding other ingredients like roasted red peppers, sun-dried tomatoes, mushrooms, or peas. You can also swap in different cheeses, such as Gorgonzola, or pasta styles such as fresh cavatelli.

tip: Pasta has a tendency to cool off quickly when piled onto a cold plate, so it's really important that the dinner plates are hot when you serve this dish. Heat them in the microwave for a minute and a half right before serving.

it's that easy: Good cheese is a real shortcut to the best flavor, but that almost always means you must buy a chunk and grate it yourself. Look for individually wrapped chunks in the gourmet cheese bin section at your grocery or visit your local cheese monger for Parmigiano-Reggiano, the king of Parmesans. Authentic Parmigiano-Reggiano has a dot matrix design on the rind. Look for a chunk with only one side of the rind (that hard inedible outer covering) attached for the best bang for your buck.

extra hungry? An escarole salad tossed with a peeled and diced navel orange, a splash of white wine vinegar, and a glug of olive oil is all you need.

in the glass: I like to drink Italian wine with Italian food, and this classic pasta would taste great with a medium-bodied Chianti. Look for the term "Riserva" on the label, as it generally denotes a higher quality.

Spinach-and-Cheese Tortellini

with LEEKS and CREAMY MUSHROOM SAUCE

Of all the shortcut products available in grocery stores, my favorite just might be fresh filled pastas. I've chosen spinach-and-cheese tortellini here because they're delicious, they cook fast, and their beautiful green color goes so well with the classic cream sauce, sweet caramelized leeks, and woodsy cremini mushrooms. The impressive sauce is surprisingly simple to make—just reduced wine and heavy cream. Yet another shortcut to making any night feel like the weekend.

2 1/2 tsp salt

14 oz/400 g fresh cheese-and-spinach tortellini

6 tsp unsalted butter, at room temperature

1 leek, white and tender green parts, trimmed, rinsed thoroughly, and thinly sliced (see "It's that easy")

1/2 tsp dried marjoram or oregano

6 oz/170 g cremini mushrooms, brushed clean and thinly sliced

1 garlic clove, minced

1/4 cup/60 ml dry white wine

1 tsp white wine vinegar

1 cup/240 ml heavy cream

Pinch of freshly grated nutmeg

Pinch of cayenne pepper

Freshly ground black pepper

2 tsp minced fresh flat-leaf parsley

1 tbsp freshly grated Parmesan cheese

1. Fill a 12-in/30.5-cm skillet with water up to about 1 in/2.5 cm from the top. Cover and bring to a boil over high heat. Add 2 tsp of the salt and toss in the tortellini. Stir gently once or twice to keep the pasta from sticking and cook, stirring occasionally, until al dente, about 5 minutes or according to the package directions. Drain the pasta in a colander set in the sink and toss with 2 tsp of the butter.

2. Return the pan to the heat, reduce the heat to medium-high, and add the remaining 4 tsp butter. When the butter is melted and hot, add the leek and marjoram and 1/4 tsp salt. Sauté until the leek begins to soften, about 1 minute. Add the mushrooms and garlic and cook until the mushrooms give off their juices, about 4 minutes. Add the wine and vinegar and cook until the pan is almost dry, about 2 minutes longer. (Raise the heat if the liquid seems to be reducing too slowly.)

3. Add the cream and bring to a simmer. The sauce should be bubbly and a little thickened in about 1 minute. Stir in the nutmeg and cayenne. Taste and add the remaining 1/4 tsp salt and a grind or two of black pepper if it needs it. Return the tortellini to the pan and toss it in the hot creamy sauce until the pasta is well coated and warmed through, about 2 minutes.

4. Scoop the tortellini into warmed shallow bowls. Scatter the parsley and Parmesan over the top and serve hot.

it's that easy: Leeks are easy to clean. Just trim off the root end and cut off and discard the tops where they turn dark green and tough. Cut the leeks in half lengthwise and rinse cold running water between the layers to remove any sand or grit. Proceed with chopping or slicing as directed.

extra hungry? How about a salad of radicchio and Bibb lettuce with a scattering of olives, a drizzle of balsamic vinegar, and a glug of olive oil?

in the glass: A Sauvignon Blanc from Oyster Bay, New Zealand, is just the thing to cut through this creamy sauce. But if you're in the mood for red, fear not. A Beaujolais or lighter-bodied Pinot Noir would be just as tasty. Look for a bottle of Mark West Pinot Noir for a surprisingly decent bottle at an economical price.

Lo Mein Noodles

with CHICKEN, SNOW PEAS, *and* PEANUT SAUCE

Peanut butter and pasta go together like, well, peanut butter and jelly—only much less sweet. This pasta favorite starts with a basic peanut dressing, but is sassed up with soy sauce, rice vinegar, brown sugar, sesame oil, and spicy chili garlic sauce. The lo mein noodles, crispy snow peas, and tender chicken breast soak up all that signature tart-and-spicy flavor we've come to love. Dinner, lunch, or even breakfast is a great time to munch on this Asian-inspired noodle dish.

3 tbsp smooth or chunky peanut butter

2 tbsp plus 1 tsp rice vinegar

2 tbsp brown sugar

1 tbsp soy sauce

1 tsp toasted sesame oil

1 tsp chili garlic sauce or red pepper flakes

1 boneless, skinless chicken breast, cut crosswise into very thin slices

Salt and freshly ground black pepper

8 oz/225 g dried lo mein noodles or linguine

1 cup/140 g snow peas

1 carrot, peeled and shredded with a julienne peeler (see "It's that easy") or grater

1 green onion, white and tender green parts, thinly sliced

2 tbsp minced fresh cilantro

1/4 cup/40 g peanuts

1. Fill a 12-in/30.5-cm skillet with water up to about 1 in/2.5 cm from the top. Cover and bring to a boil over high heat.

2. Meanwhile, in a small bowl, combine the peanut butter, rice vinegar, brown sugar, soy sauce, sesame oil, and chili garlic sauce. Using a fork, stir to mix. The mixture might not blend together that well, but that's okay. Set aside.

3. Sprinkle the chicken with salt and pepper on all sides and set aside at room temperature.

4. Add 2 tsp salt to the boiling water and toss in the lo mein noodles. Stir gently once or twice so the noodles don't stick. Cook until the noodles are about a minute shy of being completely tender, about 3 minutes. (If you're using linguine, the pasta will need about 6 minutes. To check, fish out

a strand and bite into it. It should still be chewy, but not tough.) Scoop out about 1/4 cup/60 ml of the noodle-cooking water and set it aside.

5. Quickly add the chicken and snow peas to the boiling pasta and cook until the chicken is cooked through and the snow peas are crisp-tender, about 30 seconds. Immediately drain the contents of the skillet into a colander set in the sink. Return the mixture to the hot pan and stir in the peanut sauce, carrot, green onion, and about half of the reserved pasta-cooking water. Toss with two wooden spoons or tongs until the pasta, vegetables, and chicken are all well coated with the sauce. Add a little more of the pasta water if it seems dry and/or sticky. Taste and adjust the seasoning.

6. Mound the hot noodle mixture onto warmed plates. Garnish with the cilantro and peanuts and serve hot.

it's that easy: A julienne peeler is a handy little tool. With its fine blades, it can shred a carrot into whisper-thin shards perfect for summer rolls, stir-fries, or salads. Look for it at your cookware shop or online. This useful tool is definitely worth the space it will take up in your gadget drawer. If you don't have a julienne peeler, just grate the carrot.

extra hungry? To give this meal extra heft, use two chicken breasts instead of one and cook the meat an extra 30 seconds to be sure all the pieces are cooked through.

in the glass: A Chenin Blanc from South Africa is a good choice to pair with this nutty, spicy dish. There is a range of sweetness among Chenin Blancs. Look for a fruit-driven bottle with brisk acid from producers like Graham Beck or Indaba.

Pad Thai

Every now and then I have an unrestrained need for pad thai. You know, that party of a noodle dish flecked with tart tamarind and lime, balanced by sweet honey and salty fish sauce, and all tossed together with scrambled egg, green onions, garlic, shrimp, bean sprouts, and cabbage. Like I said, it's a big party on your plate—and now you can make it yourself when you're feeling the need. Even if it's only every now and then.

4 oz/115 g rice-stick noodles, preferably Asian "L" or "M" style (see "It's that easy")

2 tbsp tamarind concentrate (see "It's that easy") or 1 ½ tbsp fresh lime juice mixed with 1 ½ tsp brown sugar

2 tbsp honey

1 tbsp fish sauce

2 tsp rice vinegar

3 tbsp vegetable oil

¼ tsp red pepper flakes

3 green onions, white and tender green parts only, thinly sliced

2 garlic cloves, minced

2 large eggs, beaten

3 cups/255 g very thinly sliced napa cabbage

6 oz/170 g cooked small shrimp

¾ cup/40 g bean sprouts

½ cup/70 g roasted salted peanuts, chopped

3 tbsp minced fresh cilantro

1 lime, ½ reserved for juice, ½ cut into wedges for garnish

Salt

1. Fill a 12-in/30.5-cm skillet with water up to about 1 in/2.5 cm from the top. Cover and bring to a boil over high heat. Add the noodles. Stir gently once or twice so the noodles don't stick. Cook until almost tender but with a little bite, about 4 minutes. Drain the noodles in a colander set in the sink and run just enough cold water over them to stop the cooking but still leave them warm.

2. Give the tamarind a stir first, if needed. In a small bowl, combine the tamarind, honey, fish sauce, rice vinegar, 1 tbsp of the vegetable oil, and the red pepper flakes and stir to mix well. Set aside.

3. Put the empty skillet over medium-high heat and add the remaining 2 tbsp vegetable oil. Add half of the green onions and all of the garlic and sauté until the garlic is fragrant, about 30 seconds. Add the eggs and scramble them into the onion-garlic mixture just until clumps form, scraping up the cooked egg from the bottom of the pan with a spatula. Stir in the cabbage and shrimp and sauté until the cabbage wilts and the shrimp are warmed through, about 30 seconds longer.

4. Quickly add the drained noodles, half of the bean sprouts, half of the peanuts, half of the cilantro, and the tamarind mixture. Toss and continue to cook until the noodles are hot and tender, about 2 minutes. Reduce the heat if the bottom of the pan threatens to scorch. Squeeze in the juice from the lime half and season with salt. Taste and adjust the seasoning.

5. Mound the pad thai on warmed plates and scatter the remaining green onions, bean sprouts, peanuts, and cilantro on top. Garnish with the lime wedges and serve hot.

it's that easy: The traditional rice-stick noodles for pad thai are about ¼ in/6 mm wide. They come in a package marked "L" or "M." You may have to go to the Asian market to find these noodles, but in a pinch, the widest rice noodles you can find at your grocery store or even spaghetti or linguine will work just fine.

Tamarind is a tart Asian fruit that adds an important flavor layer to Thai dishes. I prefer to use the concentrate because it saves time. The more traditional dried tamarind comes in a block that has to be soaked and strained through a fine mesh strainer to remove the fibers and seeds. With the tamarind concentrate, all that work has been done for you.

extra hungry? Just double the amount of shrimp in the dish to bulk it up with extra protein.

in the glass: A not-too-sweet Riesling is terrific with pad thai. Look for a bottle of Saint M Riesling from Germany.

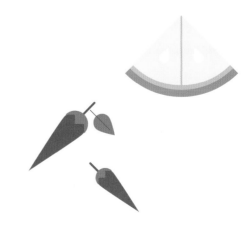

Summer Rolls

with SHRIMP, CUCUMBER, *and* MANGO

A summer roll is a fresher, leaner Thai version of a Chinese egg roll. It's essentially a salad in a rice-paper wrapper and makes a light summer meal with endless scrumptious possibilities. You can add countless vegetables and proteins, such as snow peas, red bell pepper, cabbage, chicken, and crab. You get the idea. The dipping sauce is a bright blend of lime, chile, and sugar, with just enough fish sauce to make it savory. This dish can be a popular part of a multicourse meal when entertaining—it can be fun to let your guests assemble their own summer rolls at the table. Just double or triple the ingredients to multiply your rolls as needed.

2 oz/55 g rice-stick noodles	*12 to 16 medium shrimp, peeled and deveined*
2 green onions, white and tender green parts, thinly sliced	*1/2 mango, peeled and cut into 4-in/10-cm sticks (see "It's that easy," page 89)*
1 serrano chile, minced (remove the seeds if you prefer a milder dish)	*1/2 medium seedless cucumber, peeled and cut into 4-in/10-cm sticks*
1 small garlic clove, minced	*1 carrot, peeled and grated*
1/3 cup/75 ml fresh lime juice, plus 3 tbsp (about 4 limes)	*1/2 cup/15 g fresh cilantro leaves and tender stems*
1 1/2 tbsp sugar, plus 4 tsp	*1/2 cup/10 g fresh mint leaves*
2 tbsp fish sauce, plus 4 tsp	*Six to eight 8-in/20-cm rice-paper rounds*

1. In a heatproof bowl, soak the noodles in boiling water to cover until they are softened, about 15 minutes.

2. Meanwhile, combine half of the green onions, the chile, garlic, 1/3 cup/75 ml lime juice, 1 1/2 tbsp

sugar, and 1 tbsp of the fish sauce in a medium bowl and stir to mix well. Let the sauce sit to allow the flavors to develop.

3. Drain the noodles. Combine 1 1/2 tbsp of the lime juice, 2 tsp of the sugar, and 2 tsp of the fish sauce in a medium bowl and stir to dissolve the sugar. Add the drained noodles and toss to coat them with the dressing. Set aside.

4. In a small bowl, combine the remaining 1¹/₂ tbsp lime juice, 2 tsp sugar, and 2 tsp fish sauce to make a poaching liquid for the shrimp. Heat a 12-in/ 30.5-cm skillet over medium-high heat and add the shrimp and poaching liquid. The liquid should get bubbly quickly. Toss the shrimp around in the liquid for 1 minute, then remove the pan from the heat, cover it tightly, and let the shrimp sit in the hot pan for 1 minute longer to finish cooking. Scoop the shrimp from the pan with a large slotted spoon and transfer them to a plate to cool.

5. Now you're ready to assemble the summer rolls. Arrange the noodles, shrimp, mango, cucumber, carrot, herbs, the remaining green onions, and rice-paper rounds around you on your work surface. Fill a shallow baking dish with warm water (a plate larger than the wrappers or a round platter can work, too). Soak a rice-paper round in the warm water until it begins to soften and becomes pliable, 10 to 20 seconds. Don't let it get too soft or it will be hard to handle—and remember, it will continue to soften while you fill it. Transfer the still slightly firm sheet to the work surface and lay it flat.

6. Arrange a few each of the mango and cucumber sticks, 1 tbsp or so of the carrot, a pinch of the cilantro, a few mint leaves, and green onion to taste across the bottom third of the soaked rice paper (cover an area about 5 in/12 cm wide). Lay 2 shrimp and about 3 tbsp of the noodles across the top. Fold the bottom edge of the rice paper up and over the filling and then roll it up tightly to the halfway

mark. Fold in the sides and continue to roll snugly to the end. Lay the summer roll on a plate, seam-side down. Repeat to assemble the remaining summer rolls in the same way. Since they'll stick together, arrange them on the plate so that they aren't touching.

7. Cut the rolls in half and serve with the dipping sauce.

it's that easy: Rolling up these little cylinders is a cinch. I think the most important factor in rolling success is to pull the rice-paper rounds from the water a little before they are completely pliable. They really do continue to soften as you fill them up. If you have one of the Epicurean brand cutting boards that are made of a composite material, go ahead and use that as the assembling surface. Its surface has just the right amount of stick and release.

extra hungry? Thinly slice the remaining cucumber and mango halves, arrange them on plates, and drizzle them with some of the dipping sauce (don't worry, you'll still have plenty for dipping). Sprinkle any extra herbs or a little torn basil over the top.

in the glass: Although Asian food can be a difficult match with wines, Fetzer Vineyards Valley Oak Riesling is a steal for its low price and goes nicely with the light but piquant summer rolls.

Barley and Lentil Salad
with DRIED CRANBERRIES and WALNUTS

Chewy barley and lentils are full of protein, fiber, and antioxidants, among other good things. They fill you up and keep you full for hours, meatlessly. The addition of sweet dried fruit, a zingy lemon vinaigrette, and fresh green parsley makes this salad a year-round favorite. Who knew cooking grains could be so fast and easy?

½ cup/100 g pearled barley (see "It's that easy")

½ cup/100 g dried lentils

Salt

¼ cup/40 g dried cranberries or raisins

¼ cup/55 g toasted walnuts

2 tbsp fresh lemon juice, plus more if necessary

2 tbsp olive oil

¼ cup/5 g chopped fresh flat-leaf parsley

Freshly ground black pepper

1. Add 2 cups/240 ml water, the barley, lentils, and ¼ tsp salt to a 12-in/30.5-cm skillet and bring to a simmer over medium heat. Reduce the heat to low, cover, and cook for 20 to 25 minutes or until tender, but still chewy.

2. While the grains cook, combine the cranberries, walnuts, lemon juice, olive oil, parsley, and ½ tsp salt in a medium bowl. Season with pepper.

3. When finished cooking, drain the barley-lentil mixture and add the hot grains to the cranberry mixture in the bowl. Toss to mix. Taste for seasoning and add more lemon, salt, or pepper if it needs it. Serve warm or at room temperature.

variation: You can add just about any kind of dried fruit (dried cherries, currants, figs, apricots) or nut (slivered almonds, cashews, pecans, hazelnuts) to this salad. If you have the time, try cooking up some wheat berries and add them in. Wheat berries are the entire wheat kernel (minus the hull) comprising the most nutritious sections of the bran, germ, and endosperm. They take about 45 minutes to cook, but are a delicious, healthful, and chewy addition.

it's that easy: Hulled barley is the whole-grain form of barley, with only the outermost hull removed. It's barley in its healthiest form, but it takes about an hour or more to cook. Pearled barley, which I use here, is still chewy and full of nutrition, but with the outer husk and bran layers removed so it cooks up much more quickly.

extra hungry? Anything from a rotisserie chicken to a baguette accompanied by a dish of olive oil would round out this salad beautifully.

in the glass: Let's keep it simple. If you're dining in the summer (especially outside), go for a well-chilled vinho verde like Arca Nova. If the weather is cooler, your favorite Chardonnay will be delicious.

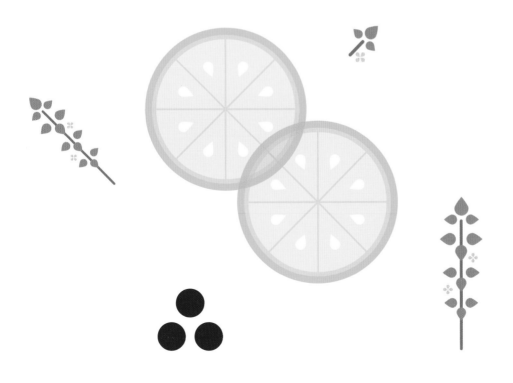

Barley Risotto

with SWEET POTATO and ANDOUILLE SAUSAGE

I love the texture of the barley in this risotto. It has a pleasant, bouncy bite that's a nice alternative to the more familiar soft and creamy Arborio-rice versions. With bright orange nuggets of sweet potato and smoky andouille sausage, this untraditional version sets you free from stirring. In order for classic risotto to be creamy, it must be stirred periodically so that the rice gives off its starch. But since barley isn't as starchy as Arborio and similar risotto rices, there's no need to stir compulsively . . . we'll just add some butter, cream, and cheese at the end to luxe it up—problem solved.

2 cups/480 ml vegetable or chicken broth

2 tbsp olive oil

2 green onions, thinly sliced, white and green parts separated

1 small sweet potato, peeled and cut into 1/4-in/6-mm dice

1 cup/200 g pearled barley

3/4 cup/140 g finely diced andouille sausage (the smoked, fully cooked variety)

Salt

3/4 cup/180 ml dry white wine

1/2 cup/55 g freshly grated Pecorino Romano cheese, plus a few shavings for garnish

2 tsp chopped fresh basil

1/4 cup/40 g frozen peas, thawed

Zest of 1 lemon

2 tbsp unsalted butter

1/4 cup/60 ml heavy cream

Freshly ground black pepper

1. Pour the vegetable broth into a large microwave-safe measuring cup and bring to a simmer in the microwave, about 3 minutes on high.

2. Heat a 12-in/30.5-cm skillet over medium-high heat and add the olive oil. When the oil shimmers, add the white parts of the green onions, the sweet potato, barley, sausage, and 1/4 tsp salt. Stir so that the kernels of barley get a little toasty. They'll change color and become kind of opaque. Cook for a few minutes, stirring every now and then, until the sausage has begun to give off a little fat, then quickly add the wine. It will bubble up. Using a wooden spoon, scrape up any bits stuck to the bottom of the pan.

3. Cook the risotto until the wine has evaporated, about 2 minutes. Add the hot broth all at once and return to a simmer. Reduce the heat to low and cook the risotto at a bare simmer for about 20 minutes. (Keep an eye on it to be sure that the pan doesn't go dry. If it gets close, add another 1/4 cup/60 ml broth or hot water.) Taste the risotto to check for doneness. The barley should be al dente and springy when you bite down on it. If it's still chalky in the center, add a little more broth or water and cook for another 3 or 4 minutes.

4. When the barley is tender, it's time to finish the risotto. Add the cheese, basil, peas, lemon zest, butter, and cream and stir until the risotto has a creamy consistency. Taste and adjust the seasoning with more salt, if needed, and pepper.

5. Scoop the risotto into warmed shallow bowls. Garnish with the reserved green onions and the cheese shavings and serve hot.

it's that easy: Instead of rice, I've lately become a fan of making risotto with barley. The grains have a delightful way of bouncing, spring-like, when you bite down on them, and cooking time isn't nearly as critical. Since barley isn't high in starch, the addition of a little cream adds that velvety quality we've come to expect in a risotto. An easy fix.

extra hungry? Serve the risotto with ciabatta bread drizzled with olive oil and coarse sea salt which has been toasted under the broiler until golden brown.

in the glass: The addition of the andouille means that you could go with a light red. My choice would be a Pinot Noir such as A to Z or King Estate Acrobat.

Lemony Risotto

with ASPARAGUS, CARROTS, *and* CHIVES

Sometimes dinner doesn't have to be a big production with meat, potato, and veg. Sometimes a creamy, dreamy risotto is just the ticket. Hot risotto warms first your mouth, and then your throat, and then spreads warm comfort all the way down into your tummy. I like to think of it as a bowl of solace. Flavored with lemon zest, chunks of green asparagus, and a confetti of sweet carrot, this spring-season risotto is more than a side dish. It's dinner.

2 tbsp unsalted butter

2 shallots, minced

1 cup/215 g Arborio rice

Salt

1/3 cup/75 ml dry white wine

15 slender asparagus spears, tough woody ends snapped off, cut into 1-in/2.5-cm pieces

1 carrot, peeled and grated

1 lemon, zested and then halved

1/2 cup/55 g freshly grated Parmesan cheese, plus a few shavings for garnish

Freshly ground black pepper

1/4 cup/60 ml heavy cream (optional)

1 tbsp minced fresh chives

1. Pour 3 cups/720 ml water into a large microwave-safe measuring cup and bring to a simmer in the microwave, about 3 minutes on high.

2. In a 12-in/30.5-cm skillet over medium heat, melt the butter. When the butter has melted and is sizzling, add the shallots and cook until they begin to soften, 1 minute or so. Add the rice and 1/2 tsp salt and sauté until the rice is opaque and smells toasty,

about 2 minutes. Add the wine (it will bubble up) and cook it until the liquid evaporates and the pan is almost dry, about 1 minute.

3. Add about 1/2 cup/120 ml of the heated water to the pan and continue cooking, stirring every now and then as the rice begins to look creamy. Reduce the heat to medium-low. Now, in spite of what you may have heard, you don't have to stand there and

continued

be a slave to your risotto. Just give it a stir every few minutes to keep it from sticking. When the water is absorbed and the mix gets thick, add another $\frac{1}{2}$ cup/120 ml of the water and cook, stirring occasionally, until absorbed. Keep adding the hot water in the same way in $\frac{1}{2}$-cup/120-ml increments, continuing to stir every now and then. Reduce the heat further if it seems to be bubbling too much. You want the risotto to simmer slowly.

4. After about 10 minutes of cooking, add the asparagus, carrot, and lemon zest and continue to cook, adding more water when the pan is drying out, until the rice and vegetables are tender, 7 to 8 minutes longer. In total you should have added about 3 cups/720 ml water.

5. Add the Parmesan and then taste, adding more salt and pepper if needed. I can't resist adding the cream at this point, but you decide if you need that luxurious boost or not. Now is the time to give the risotto a little squeeze of lemon. Add the juice from the cut half (I usually add a touch more on top of that). If the risotto seems too thick, stir in a bit more hot water. (I like my risotto a little bit on the liquidy side. Once again, it's your choice.) Taste and adjust the seasoning.

6. Spoon the hot risotto into warmed shallow bowls and garnish with the chives and Parmesan shavings. Serve hot.

it's that easy: I usually make risotto with chicken or vegetable broth, but here, I wanted the fresh springtime flavors of the asparagus and lemon to pop, and so call for plain old water, always on tap. The taste is simple, light, and clean, perfect for a warm-weather meal.

extra hungry? Pair this dish with a grocery rotisserie chicken. They are often sold by the piece, so you can buy breasts, thighs, or legs. Whatever strikes your fancy.

in the glass: Asparagus is a notoriously difficult flavor to pair with wine. Luckily for us, we have all that creamy rice, cheese, and a touch of lemon, so a citrusy Sauvignon Blanc would be just the wine for this simple meal. Look for wines with hints of grapefruit and grass in them, such as Kim Crawford Sauvignon Blanc. And don't forget to serve it a little more refreshingly chilled than you'd serve a Chardonnay.

Jambalaya

with CHICKEN, SHRIMP, and ANDOUILLE SAUSAGE

Jambalaya is the Cajun version of paella or chicken with rice. This bayou favorite from the Deep South is a mainstay at church suppers, celebrations, and wakes for a good reason: jambalaya has amazing rejuvenating powers. Whether in a giant pot to feed a hundred or a skillet to feed two, hot rice mingled with spicy juicy tomatoes, vegetables, shrimp, sausage, and chicken is the meal that holds us all together. Cue the accordion—*Jambalaya and a crawfish pie, and a filé gumbo . . . son of a gun, we'll have big fun on the bayou.*

2 tsp olive oil

4 boneless, skinless chicken thighs

3 oz/85 g andouille or other spicy smoked sausage, thinly sliced

1 small yellow onion, diced

1 green bell pepper, seeded, deribbed, and diced

1 garlic clove, minced

2 tsp Cajun seasoning (see "It's that easy")

Salt and freshly ground black pepper

½ cup/100 g white rice

One 15-oz/430-g can diced tomatoes, with juices

1 ¼ cups/300 ml chicken broth

8 medium shrimp, peeled and deveined

2 tbsp minced fresh flat-leaf parsley

Louisiana hot sauce (optional)

1. Heat a 12-in/30.5-cm skillet over medium-high heat and add the olive oil. When the oil shimmers, add the chicken thighs and brown them, about 3 minutes per side. Don't try to turn the chicken if it's stuck to the bottom of the pan; it will release once it is sufficiently browned. Transfer the chicken to a plate. (It will not be cooked through at this point.)

continued

2. Add the sausage to the hot skillet, still over medium-high heat, and cook, stirring, until nicely browned on all sides, about 1 minute. Add the onion, bell pepper, garlic, Cajun seasoning, ¼ tsp salt, and a few grinds of pepper and sauté the vegetables until they begin to soften, about 2 minutes longer. Add the rice and sauté until the grains begin to turn opaque, another minute or so.

3. Add the tomatoes with their juices and the chicken broth and return the chicken thighs to the pan, nestling them down into the liquid. Bring the mixture to a boil. Cover the pan tightly, reduce the heat to low, and simmer until the rice is tender and the chicken is cooked through, about 15 minutes. Uncover the pan, tuck the shrimp into the mix, and sprinkle the parsley over. Re-cover and cook until the shrimp is cooked through and firm to the touch, about 3 minutes more. Taste and season the jambalaya with more salt and pepper, if desired.

4. Mound the jambalaya in warmed shallow bowls and serve hot. Pass the hot sauce at the table, if desired.

it's that easy: Cajun seasoning is definitely worth having in your flavor arsenal. It has a kick, as it usually includes paprika, garlic, white pepper, and cayenne, as well as celery seed, basil, thyme, and parsley. Look for it on the grocery shelf with the other spice and herb blends. You can also add it to burgers, stews, soups, barbecue, seafood, or anything that needs a touch of attitude.

extra hungry? I can't imagine anyone still being hungry after this meal, unless you've been digging ditches all day, but a cool cucumber salad could be a welcome addition. Peel and seed a cucumber, slice it thinly, and toss it with a splash of sherry vinegar, a glug of olive oil, salt and pepper.

in the glass: Even though this dish is a blend of French and Spanish influences, I'm going to have to go with a German Riesling here. The andouille can be pretty spicy, so you're going to need a nice balance of fruit and acid. Alternatively, Australia is chiming in with some great values. Look at Plantagenet or Frisk for bottles that won't hurt your wallet.

Vegetable Biryani

with GREEN BEANS, CAULIFLOWER, *and* CARROTS

Biryani is an Asian rice pilaf scented with spices, ginger, and garlic and studded with colorful vegetables. It's often a part of a celebratory Indian meal, but it has the star power to stand alone. One of the most charming qualities of this meal is that the fragrant basmati rice kernels are distinct and not at all gooey, thanks to rinsing the rice before cooking. It's chock-full of cauliflower, carrot, and green beans and redolent of coriander, cumin, cardamom, and turmeric. In other words, it's a celebration of flavors that you'll want to devour again and again.

3/4 tsp coriander seeds

1/2 tsp cumin seeds

1/4 tsp cardamom seeds

1/4 tsp ground turmeric

1 cup/240 ml chicken broth or water

1/2 cup/120 ml milk

2 tbsp golden raisins

Salt

3/4 cup/160 g basmati rice

1/4 cup/30 g slivered almonds

2 tbsp unsalted butter

1 small yellow onion, thinly sliced

1 tbsp peeled and minced fresh ginger (see "It's that easy")

1 garlic clove, minced

1 cup/85 g cauliflower florets, cut into 1/2-in/12-mm pieces

1 carrot, peeled, halved lengthwise, and cut into 1/2-in/12-mm pieces

1 cup/140 g green beans, fresh or frozen, cut into 1-in/2.5-cm pieces

Freshly ground black pepper

1 tbsp minced fresh cilantro

1. Stir together the coriander seeds, cumin seeds, cardamom seeds, and turmeric in a small bowl. In another small bowl, combine the chicken broth, milk, raisins, and 1/2 tsp salt. Set the spice and raisin mixtures aside.

2. Rinse the rice in a strainer under cold running water, swishing it with your fingers until the water is no longer cloudy and runs clear, about 1 minute. Set aside.

3. Toast the almonds on a plate in the microwave on high for 1 minute. Stir and microwave for another 30 seconds, then stir again and microwave for 30 seconds longer. The nuts won't brown much, but will definitely taste toastier. Set them aside.

4. In a 12-in/30.5-cm skillet over medium heat, melt the butter. Add the spice mixture and let it sizzle for about 30 seconds so the spices flavor up the fat, then add the onion, ginger, and garlic and sauté until the aromatics begin to soften, about 2 minutes. Add the cauliflower, carrot, green beans, rice, broth mixture, and a few grinds of pepper and bring to a simmer. Cover, reduce the heat to low, and cook gently until the rice and vegetables are tender, about 20 minutes. Taste and season with more salt and pepper, if it needs it.

5. Scoop the biryani onto warmed plates or into shallow bowls. Garnish with the toasted almonds and cilantro and serve hot.

tip: To use up the rest of your head of cauliflower, check out Thyme-Rubbed Salmon with Shallots and Caramelized Cauliflower "Risotto" (page 166).

it's that easy: To peel fresh ginger without any fuss, just scrape the peel away with the tip of a teaspoon. It's much simpler than using a knife, and wastes less of the gingerroot as well.

extra hungry? Add 10 oz/280 g peeled, deveined shrimp during the last 5 minutes of cooking.

in the glass: The slightly sweet and floral nature of this dish pairs well with a refreshing and fruity Alsatian Gewürztraminer from Trimbach. It has the spice you're looking for, along with balanced fruit and a drier character than one often finds in lower-priced Gewürztraminers.

Mujaddara

with ONIONS, DRIED APRICOTS, ALMONDS, *and* SPICY YOGURT

Mujaddara. It's a romantic name for a simple but delicious Middle Eastern dish of caramelized onions, lentils, and fragrant jasmine rice. The caramelized onions are the standard ingredient here. They add a velvety depth to the rice and protein-packed lentils. I'd also give extra status to the spicy yogurt topping spiked with mint, lemon, and cinnamon. It adds a sophisticated twist that I find irresistible. This meal is a spice bazaar on a plate—not to mention it's healthful and filling as well.

½ cup/100 g jasmine rice

¼ cup/35 g slivered almonds

1 tbsp unsalted butter

1 tbsp olive oil

2 yellow onions, thinly sliced

Salt and freshly ground pepper

1 ¾ cups/420 ml chicken broth or water

½ cup/100 g red split lentils or green Puy lentils (see "It's that easy")

¼ cup/40 g chopped dried apricots

spicy yogurt

⅓ cup/75 g Greek yogurt

1 tbsp minced fresh mint

1 tbsp olive oil

2 tsp fresh lemon juice

1 tsp honey

¼ tsp ground cinnamon

Pinch of salt

Pinch of cayenne pepper

1. Rinse the rice in a strainer under cold running water, swishing it with your fingers until the water is no longer cloudy and runs clear, about 1 minute. Set aside.

2. Toast the almonds on a plate in the microwave on high for 1 minute. Stir and microwave for

another 30 seconds, then stir again and microwave for 30 seconds longer. The nuts won't brown much, but will definitely taste toastier. Set them aside.

3. In a 12-in/30.5-cm skillet over medium heat, melt the butter with the olive oil. When the butter is melted and hot, add the onions, ½ tsp salt, and few grinds of pepper. Sauté the onions until they soften and begin to brown, about 3 minutes. Reduce the heat to low and cook the onions, stirring, until they are tender and golden brown, about 3 minutes longer.

4. Raise the heat to medium-high and add the chicken broth and lentils, and bring to a simmer. Cover, reduce the heat to low, and simmer the lentils for 10 minutes. Uncover and stir in the apricots, rice, and almonds. Re-cover and continue to cook until the lentils and rice are almost tender, about 15 minutes longer. Remove the pan from the heat and let it sit, covered, for another 5 minutes to allow the rice and lentils to finish cooking in the steam. Taste and add more salt and pepper, if it needs it.

5. To make the spicy yogurt: Stir together the yogurt, mint, olive oil, lemon juice, honey, cinnamon, salt, and cayenne in a small bowl. Taste and adjust the seasoning. If you'd like a more drizzly sauce, stir in 1 tbsp or more water to thin it.

6. Spoon the *mujaddara* into warmed shallow bowls and top with a drizzle of the yogurt sauce before serving.

it's that easy: I get my red split and small green Puy lentils (sometimes called French lentils) at the health-food store down the street. Italian markets will often carry the green ones and the Middle Eastern markets will have the red split ones for sure. If that is too much trouble, just buy the brown ones on your local grocery shelf. The color won't be as nice, but they will be just as delicious.

extra hungry? At times, my husband balks at the idea of a meatless meal. That's when I pick up a rotisserie chicken (or just pieces of one) to boost the portion on his plate. It's a very simple solution for those times when our appetites don't exactly match up. Or if you're both feeling a little hungrier tonight, you can add four boneless, skinless chicken thighs, cut into bite-size pieces, to the stew when you add the rice. It's an almost effortless addition of protein to the meal.

in the glass: The lentils dictate a simple, light red like a Beaujolais from Georges DuBoeuf. His *Fleurie Domaine des Quatre Vents 2009* was a hit for us, but any Beaujolais from Duboeuf would be très magnifique.

Croque Madame

Croque Madame is a heavenly little grilled ham, cheese, and egg sandwich served in bistros all over France. What makes this sandwich different from the grilled cheese your mom used to make is that it is slathered in béchamel sauce and topped with a fried egg. These upscale additions remove *la croque* from the lunch category and take it firmly to the dinner-worthy column. I think Mom would approve.

½ cup/155 g unsalted butter,
at room temperature

4 slices fresh, crusty artisan bread
(see "It's that easy),
each about ½ in/12 mm thick

2 tbsp Dijon mustard

4 slices Gruyère or Swiss cheese

4 oz/115 g Black Forest ham, thinly sliced

1 ripe plum tomato, thinly sliced

Salt and freshly ground black pepper

2 large eggs

1 tbsp all-purpose flour

¾ cup/180 ml milk,
warmed in the microwave

1. Spread about 1 tbsp of the butter on one side of each bread slice. Turn them butter-side down and spread the other sides with the mustard. Top two of the slices with one slice of cheese on the mustard side. Arrange half of the ham on each cheese slice, followed by a layer of tomato and a sprinkle of salt and pepper. Finish with the remaining two cheese slices, one on each, and close the sandwiches with the two remaining bread slices, butter-side up.

2. Heat a 12-in/30.5-cm skillet over medium heat. When it's hot, add the sandwiches to the pan and brown them on the first side, about 4 minutes. If they are browning too fast, reduce the heat—you want the heat to reach the inside of the sandwich so that the ham is hot and the cheese is melted, without burning the bread. Using a wide spatula, carefully flip the sandwiches over and brown the second sides, about 3 minutes longer. They should be crispy and crunchily browned. Transfer to warmed plates.

3. Add 2 tbsp of the butter to the hot pan and raise the heat to medium-high. When the butter is melted and begins to sizzle, break the eggs gently into the pan and sprinkle them with salt and pepper.

Fry the eggs just until they are set, about 1 minute, then give them a gentle flip with a spatula and cook the other side for another minute. Try not to break the yolks so they're still a little runny on the inside. Transfer the eggs to a separate warmed plate and cover to keep warm.

4. Scrape out any crunchy egg remaining in the pan and discard it. Add the remaining butter to the hot pan and when the butter is melted, add the flour, 1/4 tsp salt, and a few grinds of pepper and stir until the flour foams, about 30 seconds. Whisk in the warm milk and continue to cook the sauce until it boils and thickens, about 1 minute. Remove the sauce from the heat and pour it over the sandwiches. Top them with the fried eggs and serve hot.

variation: Swiss, Cheddar, fontina, Monterey Jack . . . literally any melting cheese will work in this sandwich. Also feel free to use any sliced meats like roast beef, corned beef, prosciutto, turkey, et cetera. Other spreads like horseradish, mayonnaise, and flavored mustards are fun ways to experiment as well.

it's that easy: When it comes to sandwiches, bread is usually the main ingredient, so buy the best bread you can find. The price difference between a so-so loaf and a really good artisan loaf is minimal, so it is worth the splurge. Artisan breads don't usually contain preservatives, so to keep fresh, store the sliced bread in the freezer and remove it by the slice when you need it.

extra hungry? A petite salade *of pickled vegetables would be a welcome addition to this sandwich meal. You can find them at the grocery in multiple combinations (think cauliflower, carrots, onions, peppers), spicy or not, in glass jars near where the olives are displayed.*

in the glass: Look for a white wine with low acid and a hint of sweetness, like a Müller-Thurgau from the Alto Adige in Italy or Alsace, France.

Cuban Sandwiches

This hot sandwich is a complete meal wrapped between two slices of bread. I love the combination of tart pickles, salty ham, and gooey hot cheese but the pork in this sandwich really makes it sing. Slow-cooked shredded pork can be purchased in the deli section of most markets or it can be found packaged in the refrigerated meat sections. Just look for it. It makes an epic sandwich like this possible. Oink, oink.

2 hoagie rolls or French rolls, split

1 tbsp unsalted butter, at room temperature

2 tbsp mustard of your choice

6 slices ham (see Tip)

4 slices Swiss cheese

6 pickle rounds or 2 large pickles, cut lengthwise into ¼-in/6-mm slices

2/3 cup/115 g shredded roast pork shoulder or 6 slices deli roast pork

1. Lay the rolls cut-side down on a work surface. Butter the outsides generously with the butter. Turn them butter-side down and spread the mustard on cut sides. Layer the ham, cheese, pickles, and pork on the sandwich bottoms, dividing them evenly. Replace the tops, butter-side out.

2. Heat a 12-in/30.5-cm skillet over medium-high heat. When the pan is hot, carefully add the buttered sandwiches, top-side down. Weight the sandwiches with a brick wrapped in aluminum foil (see "It's that easy") or another heavy pan. Cook until browned and crispy on the first side, about 3 minutes. Reduce the heat if they threaten to brown too fast—you want the inside of the sandwich to be warmed through and the cheese oozing before the bread chars. Flip the sandwiches over and cook the second side for another 2 or 3 minutes until browned. Remove the sandwiches from the pan, cut in half, and serve hot.

tip: The better the ham, the better the sandwich. Black Forest is delicious.

it's that easy: You don't need no stinkin' panini press. A foil-wrapped brick can do the job just as well. It compresses the meaty, juicy insides while helping the exterior crisp up to crunchy browned perfection. Now go ahead and give yourself a pat on the back, because you've just MacGyver'd a do-it-yourself panini press for creating great tasting, crispy-hot sandwiches at home.

extra hungry? How about a pile of sea salt kettle-fried potato chips? You know you love them.

in the glass: There is something fabulous about a cold beer with a hot sandwich. A Dos Equis from Mexico or a bottle of your current favorite brew would pair well with the pickles, mustard, and ham in this zesty sandwich.

START TO FINISH
35 minutes
...
HANDS-ON TIME
35 minutes
...
serves 2

Fried Green Tomato Sandwiches

with BACON *and* CHUTNEY

Most everyone gets excited about ripe summer tomatoes. But I'm addicted to the unripened green ones! Especially when they're fried up crispy in a hot, hot pan of bacon fat. And they're even more delectable when paired with creamy avocado, crunchy iceberg lettuce, salty bacon, and tucked inside a toasted English muffin spread with tart-sweet Major Grey's chutney. This meal, a harmonious blend of rebel yell and Union Jack, is definitely something to get excited about.

3/4 cup/85 g panko bread crumbs

1/4 cup/30 g all-purpose flour

1 large egg

1 green tomato, cut into 4 big slices 1/2 in/12 mm thick

Salt and freshly ground black pepper

8 slices bacon

1 tbsp vegetable oil, or as needed (optional)

1/3 cup/100 g Major Grey's chutney

4 English muffins, split and toasted

1/2 ripe avocado, peeled and thinly sliced (see "It's that easy")

4 or 8 iceberg lettuce leaves

1. Put the panko and flour in two separate shallow bowls. Put the egg in a third shallow bowl and beat until well blended. Sprinkle the tomato slices on both sides with salt and pepper and dredge them in the flour, shaking off the excess. Dip the slices in the egg and then dredge them in the panko to coat completely. Set aside on a plate.

2. Heat a 12-in/30.5-cm skillet over medium-high heat and add half the bacon slices. Cook, turning as needed, until crispy, 5 to 7 minutes total. Transfer to paper towels to drain. Cook the remaining bacon in the same way.

continued

THE CARBOHYDRATE CURE

from the microwave, stir to dissolve the sugar, and immediately add the cucumber, pushing it down so that all the slices are completely submerged in the liquid. Let the cucumber pickle for at least 10 minutes and up to 30 minutes, then drain and set aside to cool.

3. In a large bowl, combine the tuna, celery, bell pepper, cilantro, garlic, egg, 1/2 cup/55 g of the panko, the lemon juice, the remaining 1/2 tsp salt, a few grinds of black pepper, and the cayenne. Toss the mixture gently with your hands until thoroughly combined. Shape the tuna mixture into two burgers no more than 1 in/2.5 cm thick. Refrigerate for 20 minutes to firm up.

4. Meanwhile, preheat the broiler. Brush the cut sides of the buns with the melted butter. Slip the buns under the broiler and toast until golden, about 1 minute.

5. Stir together the mayonnaise and wasabi powder in a small bowl until well blended. Taste. The spread may be hot enough for you at this point. If you want more heat, continue to add wasabi powder in small amounts until you get it right. If the powder is lumpy, press it through a small strainer before adding it to the mayo.

6. Pour the remaining 1/2 cup/55 g panko onto a plate. Remove the tuna burgers from the fridge and coat with the panko on each side, pressing to adhere.

7. Heat a 12-in/30.5-cm skillet over medium-high heat and add the vegetable oil. When it shimmers, add the burgers to the pan and fry until crispy and brown on the first side, about 4 minutes. Turn the burgers and cook until browned on the second side and firm to the touch when pressed lightly with your finger, about 3 minutes longer. If you want your tuna burger a bit more on the rare side, cook it for 3 minutes on the first side and 2 minutes on the second.

8. Serve the burgers on the toasted buns, spread with the wasabi mayonnaise, and topped with the cucumber pickle, avocado slices, and arugula.

variations: In place of the pickle and wasabi mayo, try other things atop these burgers, such as Asian slaw, mango salsa, pico de gallo, Major Grey's chutney, bread and butter pickles, chimichurri, cilantro chutney, onion marmalade, et cetera. Many of these additions are available on the grocery store shelf, so all you have to do is open a jar.

it's that easy: This dish is a good use for the packaged frozen tuna steaks found in your grocery store. No need to buy the fresh stuff, since you're adding many flavor enhancers and maybe even cooking it up beyond medium-rare.

extra hungry? Serve this tuna burger with your favorite chips. Mine are the kettle-fried salt-and-vinegar variety.

in the glass: Gewürztraminer—there are so many styles inherent in this palate-pleasing German wine, from spicy and lively to dry to soft. This varietal goes well with spicy foods and is a favorite to pair with Chinese, Thai, or Indian fare.

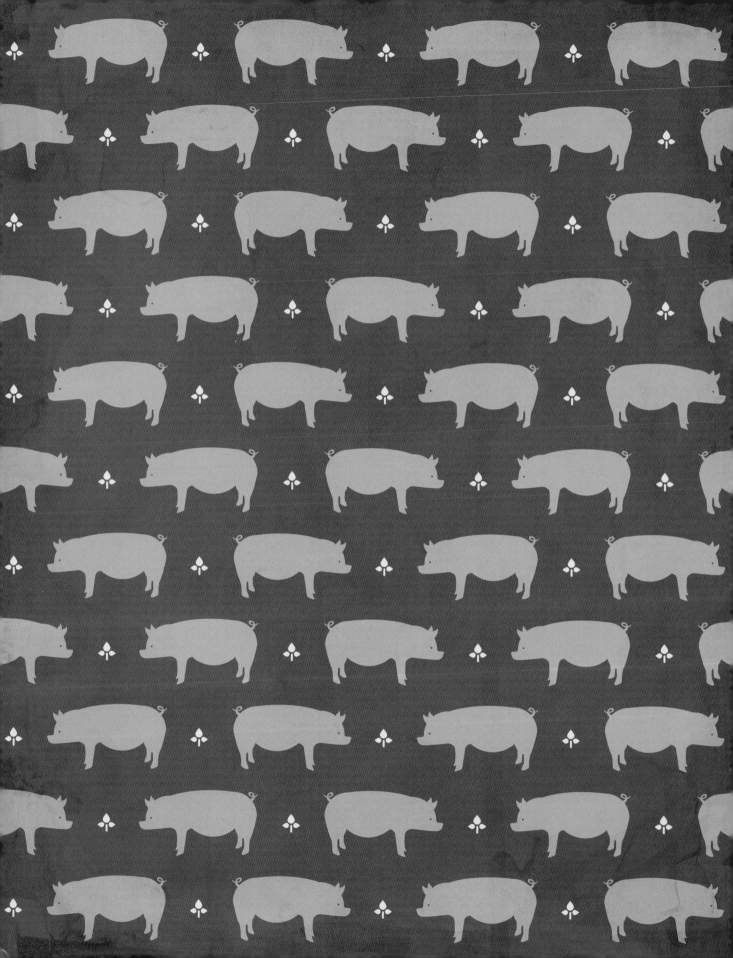

CHAPTER

2

meat dinners

Quick Choucroute Garni

Choucroute garni is an Alsatian dish of sauerkraut, potatoes, spices, and any number of pork products, from a pig's shoulder to his knuckles. I've kept it simple here with bacon, kielbasa, and sauerkraut, but it just wouldn't be the classic dish without the addition of clove, allspice, and wine with a diced apple tossed in for good measure. Don't forget to slather mustard or horseradish on the sausages and potatoes at the table. I'm always surprised at how good this meal tastes. Sometimes simple really is best.

2 whole cloves

2 whole allspice

1 bay leaf, crumbled

1/2 tsp salt

1/2 cup/120 ml dry white wine

1/2 cup/120 ml chicken broth

1 tbsp olive oil

2 slices bacon, diced

1 small yellow onion, thinly sliced

1 tart-sweet apple such as Braeburn or Crispin, peeled, cored, and cut into 1/2-in/12-mm dice

2 new potatoes, scrubbed and cut into 1/2-in/12-mm dice

10 oz/280 g kielbasa, knockwurst, or bratwurst or a combination, cut into 2-in/5-cm pieces

1 lb/455 g sauerkraut, drained and squeezed dry (see "It's that easy")

Freshly ground black pepper

2 tsp minced fresh flat-leaf parsley

Whole-grain mustard and prepared horseradish for serving

1. In a bowl, combine the cloves, allspice, bay leaf, salt, wine, and chicken broth. Set aside.

2. Heat a 12-in/30.5-cm skillet over medium-high heat and add the olive oil. When the oil shimmers, add the bacon and cook, stirring, it until it renders its fat and is almost crispy, about 3 minutes. Add the onion, apple, and potatoes and sauté until the onion is softened, about 3 minutes. Add the kielbasa, spiced broth mixture, sauerkraut, and a few grinds of pepper and stir it all together. Bring to a simmer, cover, and reduce the heat to low. Simmer the choucroute until the flavors have blended and the potatoes are tender, about 20 minutes.

3. Mound the choucroute onto two warmed plates and sprinkle the parsley over the top. Serve hot, with the mustard and horseradish on the side.

it's that easy: The trick to making great-tasting sauerkraut dishes is squeezing out most of the super-tart sauerkraut juice and replacing it with a mix of chicken broth and wine. It mellows the tartness factor, making it a more pleasant dish.

extra hungry? To make this dish dinner-worthy, I include bacon and kielbasa sausage, but if you're in the mood and super-hungry, go ahead and add a diced smoked pork chop or diced ham to "pork" it up.

in the glass: Look for a dry Riesling from Alsace, such as Trimbach, for a good balance between sweet and acid.

Braised Lentils

with POLISH KIELBASA and CABBAGE

When looking for a hearty meal, look no further than this dish. It's full of vegetables, earthy lentils, and garlicky kielbasa sausage, simmered in chicken broth and scented with rosemary. Not only are lentils delicious and fast-cooking, they are packed full of protein and fiber—good for helping keep you full for an action-packed evening. This is a classic weeknight meal: simple, healthful, and delicious, using items that are on hand in the pantry and refrigerator.

1 tbsp vegetable oil

1 small yellow onion, thinly sliced

2 cups/170 g thinly sliced cabbage

1 carrot, peeled and thinly sliced

1/2 celery stalk, thinly sliced

1 garlic clove, minced

2 tsp minced fresh rosemary or 1 tsp dried

1/2 tsp salt

Freshly ground black pepper

1/3 cup/75 ml dry white wine or apple juice

3/4 cup/150 g dried lentils (see "It's that easy")

1 1/4 cups/300 ml chicken broth

8 oz/225 g Polish kielbasa, cut into bite-size pieces

2 tsp minced fresh flat-leaf parsley

1. Heat a 12-in/30.5-cm skillet over medium-high heat and add the vegetable oil. When the oil shimmers, add the onion and sauté until it begins to soften, about 1 minute. Add the cabbage, carrot, celery, garlic, rosemary, salt, and a grind or two of pepper and sauté until the vegetables begin to soften, about 3 minutes.

2. Pour in the wine and cook, stirring, it until it has almost cooked off, about 1 minute. Add the lentils,

chicken broth, and kielbasa and stir, using your spoon to push on the lentils so they are immersed in the liquid. Bring to a simmer. Cover, reduce the heat to low, and simmer gently until the lentils are tender, about 25 minutes. Taste and adjust the seasoning.

3. Mound the lentils, vegetables, and sausage on two warmed plates, garnish with the parsley, and serve hot.

it's that easy: *The lentils on your grocery store shelf are probably the everyday brown variety, but there are other lovely types as well. Look for red, yellow, green French lentils (lentilles du Puy), or the little black lentils called "beluga" for an exotic change of pace. They're fairly interchangeable and cook in about the same amount of time.*

extra hungry? *For an even more filling meal, add toasted baguette rounds spread with goat cheese and topped with a sun-dried tomato.*

in the glass: *A creamy, chilled Chardonnay would be a delicious complement to the rich flavors of this hearty dinner. For a fine bottle for everyday drinking, look for New Zealand's Babich Hawke's Bay Unoaked Chardonnay.*

Golden Corn Cakes

with CRISPY PANCETTA and ARUGULA SALAD

Temptation, thy name is corn cake. Especially when paired with crispy Italian bacon and lemony dressed arugula salad. I've got to admit, I love making this dish when fresh corn is king, but it's also delicious with frozen corn, when winter-weary palates yearn for a flash of summer on the plate. Thanks to Yotam Ottolenghi for inspiration for this dish.

1 green onion, white and tender green parts, thinly sliced

1/2 jalapeño chile, seeded and minced

2 tbsp thinly sliced fresh basil

Kernels from 4 ears corn or 2 cups/340 g frozen corn, thawed (see "It's that easy")

1/4 cup/35 g cornmeal

3 tbsp all-purpose flour

1/4 tsp ground cumin

Salt and freshly ground black pepper

1/2 cup/120 ml whole-fat plain Greek yogurt, plus more for topping

1 large egg

3 tbsp olive oil, plus more for frying

2 tsp fresh lemon juice

8 slices pancetta or 3 slices bacon

2 handfuls arugula

1. In a medium bowl, combine the green onion, jalapeño, basil, corn, cornmeal, flour, cumin, 1/4 tsp salt, and a few grinds of black pepper. In a large bowl, whisk together the 1/2 cup/120 ml yogurt, egg, and 1 tbsp of the olive oil. Add the dry ingredients and stir just until a thick batter comes together.

2. In another medium bowl, whisk together the lemon juice, 1 tbsp olive oil, a pinch of salt, and a grind of pepper for the salad dressing. Set aside.

3. Heat a 12-in/30.5-cm skillet over medium-high heat and add the remaining 1 tbsp oil and the pancetta. Cook the pancetta without disturbing until it's crispy on one side, about 2 minutes. Turn with tongs and cook until crisp all over, about 1 minute longer. (If using regular bacon, it will take more like 5 to 7 minutes, turning as needed, to crisp.) Remove from the heat. Using a slotted spoon, scoop the pancetta onto a paper towel–lined plate to drain. When it's cooled, crumble and set aside.

4. There should be enough fat in the pan, but add enough olive oil to give the bottom a good coating, if needed. Return the pan to medium-high heat and heat until blazing hot. Add the corn batter in 1/3-cup/75-ml portions. You should be able to fit four scoops in the pan. Flatten the mounds of batter with the back of a fork and tidy up the sides with the tines. Cook until golden on the bottom, 2 to 3 minutes. Using a thin-edged spatula, flip the cakes over and cook until they're golden on the second side, about 1 minute longer. (The corn kernels might pop, so don't be startled!) Transfer the cakes as they are done to a paper towel–lined plate. Repeat to cook the remaining batter, adding more oil to the pan as needed.

5. Whisk the lemon dressing if it has separated and add the arugula, tossing to coat it. Arrange the dressed salad on two warmed plates and top it with the hot corn cakes, a dollop of yogurt, and the crumbled pancetta. Serve hot. The greens will wilt a little bit, but that's a good thing.

it's that easy: *If you're using frozen corn for this dish, splurge on the baby gold and white variety—it's sweeter, more tender, and less starchy. If using fresh corn, it's easy to cut the corn from the ears. Grab your biggest bowl and hold the ear of corn in it, small end pointing up. Hold the corn with one hand and, holding a sharp knife in your other hand, cut down along the cob, following the contours and keeping the knife close to the cob to get the whole kernels and their juices. Using the bowl helps to keep stray corn kernels from bouncing all over the kitchen.*

extra hungry? *This is a light meal, perfect for a summer dinner on the patio. For hungry appetites, add a classic shrimp cocktail on the side. Purchase cooked shrimp from the fish case at the market along with the already-mixed-up cocktail sauce of your choice. Serve it with a few lemon wedges for squeezing.*

in the glass: *I was seeking something white, light, and fruity for this wine pairing, and remembered nothing satisfies those terms like a bottle of vinho verde from Portugal. The Gazela label delivers delicate white-fruit aromas and light carbonation along with crisp, dry flavor.*

Crispy Sage Pork Cutlets

with COUSCOUS, PEAS, FIGS, and PISTACHIOS

When sage is fried in butter, it changes from a rough, sometimes overpowering herb into a sophisticated, hard-to-define kind of delicious. I love how the sage's flavor infuses the butter in the pan, which is then used to fry up the pork chops so that sage flavor and aroma perfumes the pork cutlets as well. The peas, figs, and pistachios flavor the couscous with sweetness, crunch, and color. What more could you ask from dinner?

12 oz/340 g pork cutlets, about 1/4 in/6 mm thick

Salt and freshly ground black pepper

2 tbsp unsalted butter

12 fresh sage leaves

1 small yellow onion, diced

1 carrot, peeled and thinly sliced

3/4 cup/180 ml chicken broth

5 dried Calimyrna or Mission figs, stemmed and quartered

1 green onion, white and tender green parts, thinly sliced

2/3 cup/115 g couscous (see "It's that easy")

1/2 cup/70 g frozen peas

1/4 cup/30 g shelled pistachios

2 tbsp extra-virgin olive oil

1. Sprinkle the pork cutlets with salt and pepper on both sides. Set aside.

2. In a 12-in/30.5-cm skillet over medium-high heat, add 1 tbsp of the butter. When it's melted, add the sage leaves and brown them on both sides until they are crispy, about 1 minute total. They should bubble and the butter should become golden brown. Reduce the heat if the butter starts to burn. Using

tongs, transfer the sage leaves to a paper towel–lined plate to drain.

3. Quickly add the pork cutlets to the hot pan and brown on the first side for 2 minutes. Turn and brown the second side for another 2 minutes. Transfer the pork to a plate and tent with aluminum foil to keep warm.

continued

4. Again working quickly, add the remaining 1 tbsp butter, the yellow onion, carrot, 1/4 tsp salt, and a sprinkle of pepper to the hot pan and sauté until the onion begins to soften, about 1 minute. Add the chicken broth and figs and bring to a simmer. Cook for 1 minute, then add the green onion, couscous, peas, and pistachios. Stir to moisten all of the couscous. Cover tightly and remove the pan from the heat. Allow the couscous to steam and absorb the broth until tender, about 4 minutes. Drizzle the olive oil over the top and stir it in. Taste the couscous and season with more salt and pepper if it needs it.

5. Arrange the pork cutlets on two warmed plates and top with the crispy sage leaves. Mound the couscous and vegetables on the side. Serve hot.

it's that easy: *Couscous is easy to pair up with endless main course options because it's a blank canvas. Just add flavors that you like: nuts, dried fruits, roasted vegetables, herbs, spices, and any broth can be incorporated into the couscous base. Once you become acquainted with this tender, tiny pasta, you'll think of all kinds of ways to make it interesting.*

extra hungry? *A green salad of romaine lettuce with tomato, cucumber, a squirt of lemon, a glug of olive oil, and few shavings of Parmesan would round out this fall meal very nicely.*

in the glass: *My preference for reds comes out in this one—especially when it's so easy to find an affordable Côtes du Rhône to open up on a Tuesday night. In my humble opinion, Côtes du Rhône makes every night a party, and an inexpensive bottling from E. Guigal or Parallèle 45 makes any meal just that much more special.*

Sautéed Pork Chops

with SWEET POTATO, APPLE, *and* MUSTARD SAUCE

The classic combination of tender pork, tart apples, and cider-braised sweet potatoes is a text-book meal for chilly days, especially when you're really hungry. You'll be amazed how easy it is to pull this hearty meal together; even the cider-based mustard sauce is a snap to prepare.

½ cup/120 ml apple cider or juice, plus more if needed

¼ tsp ground cinnamon

Salt

2 boneless, center-cut loin pork chops, about ¾ in/2 cm thick

Freshly ground black pepper

2 tbsp olive oil

1 medium sweet potato, about ½ lb/225 g, peeled and very thinly sliced

1 Braeburn, Gala, or other sweet-tart apple, cored and thinly sliced

1 shallot, minced

1 tsp Dijon mustard, smooth or whole-grain (see "It's that easy")

2 tsp minced fresh flat-leaf parsley

1. Combine the cider, cinnamon and ¼ tsp salt in a cup. Set aside.

2. Pat the pork chops dry and sprinkle all over with salt and pepper.

3. Heat a 12-in/30.5-cm skillet over medium-high heat and add the olive oil. When the oil shimmers, add the seasoned pork chops to the pan and cook until lightly browned on the first side, about 3 minutes. Turn and cook until browned on the second side, about 2 minutes longer. Transfer the pork chops to a plate. (They will not be cooked through at this point.)

4. Add the sweet potato, apple, shallot, cider mixture, and a grind or two of pepper to the hot pan. Bring it all to a simmer, cover, and reduce the heat to medium-low or low—the pan should bubble, but not too aggressively. Cook the potato mixture until a fork easily pierces the partially cooked potato but there is still some resistance, about 10 minutes.

continued

5. Return the pork chops to the pan (along with any juices accumulated on the plate) and nestle them into the potatoes and apples. Cover and cook until the meat is cooked through and the potatoes are tender, about 8 minutes longer. Taste and adjust the seasoning.

6. Transfer the pork chops, potatoes, and apples to two warmed plates. There should be some liquid remaining in the pan to serve as a base for the sauce. (If the potatoes have absorbed all of the liquid, add 2 to 3 tbsp cider to the pan and heat it briefly over medium heat.) Stir the mustard into the pan juices with a fork. Taste the sauce and add more pepper if it needs it.

7. Spoon the sauce over the meat and vegetables, sprinkle the parsley over the top, and serve hot.

it's that easy: *Pardon me, but, do you have any Grey Poupon? If not, get some, or purchase one of the many exceptional whole-grain mustards on the grocery shelves these days—they have more "pow!" than the smooth Dijon style. Pommery Moutarde de Meaux is the gold standard, having been "served at the tables of French kings since 1632," which probably makes it good enough for the rest of us.*

extra hungry? *Add steam-in-the-bag peas for a welcome splash of green on the plate.*

in the glass: *A medium-dry Riesling will complement the sweet pork and apples, as would a tall, cold glass of Belgian-style wheat ale such as Blue Moon.*

Herb-Rubbed Pork

with HONEY-LIME ROASTED SWEET POTATOES, CAULIFLOWER, *and* MAJOR GREY'S CHUTNEY

Pork tenderloin is indeed tender as well as juicy and flavorful when cooked just until rosy and pink in the center. Especially so when rubbed with herbes de Provence, an herb blend from, you guessed it, Provence. Thyme, rosemary, basil, fennel, and marjoram are the main flavors, so if you can't find it just blend up a mixture of your own. The lime-and-honey–glazed sweet potatoes and cauliflower are addictive when paired with the pork and Major Grey's, the beloved mango-based chutney.

10 oz/280 g pork tenderloin, trimmed (see "It's that easy") and cut in half lengthwise (so it cooks faster)

Salt and freshly ground black pepper

3 tbsp olive oil

2 tsp dried herbes de Provence or a mixture of equal parts dried thyme, rosemary, fennel, marjoram, and basil

2 tbsp honey

1 tbsp fresh lime juice

1/2 tsp ground cinnamon

1 medium sweet potato, about 1/2 lb/225 g, peeled, cut in half lengthwise, and then cut crosswise into slices about 1/8 in/3 mm thick

2 cups/200 g thinly sliced cauliflower florets

1/4 cup/40 g raisins

2 tbsp dry white wine or chicken broth

Major Grey's chutney for serving

2 tsp minced fresh flat-leaf parsley

1. Preheat the oven to 425°F/220°C/gas 7.

2. Season the tenderloin with salt and pepper and rub it all over with 1 tbsp of the olive oil. Sprinkle the herbes de Provence all over the pork and press to help stick to the meat. In a small bowl, stir together the honey, lime juice, and cinnamon. Set the pork and the glaze aside.

3. Heat a 12-in/30.5-cm ovenproof skillet over medium-high heat and add the remaining 2 tbsp olive oil. When the oil shimmers, add the sweet potato and cauliflower, 1/2 tsp salt, and a few grinds of pepper and toss the vegetables to coat them with the oil and seasoning. Drizzle in the honey mixture and toss the vegetables to coat them evenly. They should begin to sizzle.

4. Transfer the vegetables to the oven and roast for 7 minutes. Remove the skillet from the oven and stir in the raisins (the vegetables won't be tender yet). Lay the tenderloin pieces on top of the vegetables and return the skillet to the oven until the tenderloin is medium-rare, about 15 minutes—it should still be rosy in the center, and an instant-read thermometer will read 145°F/60°C when inserted into the thickest part. Remove the skillet from the oven (be careful, as the handle will be blazing hot). Transfer the meat to a cutting board and let rest for 3 or 4 minutes to allow the juices to redistribute before carving. Meanwhile, place the skillet over medium-high heat and add the wine. Cook, stirring up the vegetables, until the wine reduces a little, 1 or 2 minutes. Taste and adjust the seasoning.

5. Cut the tenderloin crosswise on the diagonal into slices about 1 in/2.5 cm thick. Arrange the slices on two warmed plates and pile the vegetables and a scoop of chutney on the side. Sprinkle with the parsley and serve hot.

it's that easy: Pork tenderloins are often sold with the tough, sinewy covering called "silver skin" still attached, and it must be removed before cooking. To do so, cut under the edge of the rubbery translucent outer layer with the tip of a sharp knife and slice down just between the sinew and meat to slice away the tough part. Try not to lose too much meat in the process, but don't worry—you definitely get better at it with practice. Or ask your butcher to do it for you.

extra hungry? Just add warm cornbread from your local bakery with softened sweet butter.

in the glass: How about an easy-to-drink Albariño from Spain. This white varietal is inexpensive, light, and fruity . . . a perfect pairing with this pork and sweet potato dish.

Spicy Pork Stir-Fry

with LIME, CASHEWS, *and* NOODLES

Stir-fries are a great way to get dinner on the table fast, with the added bonus that they're healthful *and* delicious. There's so much to love about this meal full of crispy snow peas, buttery cashews, and tender pork with a hint of lime. And the noodles . . . I can't resist pork and silky hot noodles bathed in sesame sauce, and I bet you won't be able to, either.

2 tbsp fresh lime juice

2 tbsp soy sauce

2 tbsp sesame oil, plus 1 tsp

3/4 tsp cornstarch

2 tsp honey

2 tsp chili garlic sauce

8 oz/225 g boneless pork tenderloin (see "It's that easy"), silver skin removed if necessary (see "It's that easy," page 83), thinly sliced, and then cut crosswise into strips

2 tsp salt

4 oz/115 g udon or lo mein noodles

2 tbsp vegetable oil

1 tbsp peeled and minced fresh ginger

2 garlic cloves, minced

1 red bell pepper, seeded, deribbed, and cut into 1/4-in/6-mm strips

4 oz/115 g snow peas, trimmed and cut in half

1 green onion, white and tender green parts, thinly sliced

1/3 cup/50 g salted cashews

1. Fill a 12-in/30.5-cm skillet with water up to about 1 in/2.5 cm from the top. Cover and bring to a boil over high heat.

2. In a bowl, whisk together the lime juice, soy sauce, 2 tbsp sesame oil, cornstarch, honey, and chili garlic sauce. Add the pork and toss to coat it well.

3. Add the salt to the boiling water and toss in the noodles. Cook until al dente, about 10 minutes or according to the package directions. (To check, fish out a strand and bite into it. It should still be chewy, but not tough.) Drain the noodles in a colander set in the sink and toss them with the 1 tsp sesame oil to coat the noodles and help keep them from sticking.

4. Put the skillet over medium-high heat and add the vegetable oil. When the oil shimmers, add the ginger, garlic, bell pepper, and snow peas and stir-fry until the vegetables are crisp-tender, about 4 minutes. Add the pork with its marinade and stir-fry it until it is no longer pink in the center and the sauce thickens, about 1 minute. Add the noodles and toss the mixture until it's thoroughly heated through, about 2 minutes.

5. Mound the noodles, meat, and vegetables onto two warmed plates. Sprinkle the green onion and cashews over the top and serve hot.

it's that easy: Most pork tenderloins are about 1 lb/ 455 g, so you're going to use about half of a whole tenderloin. You can freeze the remaining meat to use at a later date. For example, this dish is so good, you'll probably make it again soon.

extra hungry? Add about 1 cup/140 g thawed frozen edamame to the veggie sauté along with the other vegetables for an extra protein kick.

in the glass: The spicy nature of this dish dictates a Gewürztraminer. Look for Snoqualmie Vineyards Gewürztraminer Naked. It's actually quite dry, with just a whisper of sweetness.

Spicy Orange Beef Stir-Fry

with SNOW PEAS and CARROTS

I think it's fair to say that growing up in West Virginia in the '60s, there weren't lots of gastronomic opportunities. But my family did eat out frequently at a local Chinese restaurant, where my developing palate quickly became hooked on the exotic tastes and textures of Cantonese-American cuisine. If you, like me, have a regular and unrelenting hankering for spicy orange beef, you're going to love being able to make this citrusy dish at home. The flavors are fresh and bright, and this version is *waaaay* healthier than the usual restaurant plate, since the meat is simply cooked up with the vegetables instead of deep-fried.

8 oz/225 g beef sirloin, thinly sliced into 3-in/7.5-cm strips

2 tbsp soy sauce, plus more if needed

Freshly ground black pepper

Zest and juice of 1 orange (see "It's that easy")

1 tbsp dry white wine

1 tbsp hoisin sauce

1 tbsp sugar

1 tsp cornstarch

1 tsp toasted sesame oil

1 tsp chili garlic sauce, plus more if needed

2 tbsp vegetable oil

1 tbsp peeled and minced fresh ginger

1 garlic clove, minced

2 carrots, peeled and thinly sliced

2 green onions, white and tender green parts, thinly sliced

2 cups/280 g snow peas

Microwave steam-in-the-bag rice for serving

2 tbsp minced fresh cilantro

1. In a medium bowl, toss the sliced meat with 1 tbsp of the soy sauce and a few grinds of black pepper. Set aside at room temperature.

2. In a small bowl, combine the orange zest and juice, wine, hoisin sauce, sugar, cornstarch, sesame oil, chili garlic sauce, and remaining 1 tbsp soy sauce and mix well to make a stir-fry sauce. Set aside.

3. Heat a 12-in/30.5-cm skillet over medium-high heat and add 1 tbsp of the vegetable oil. When the oil shimmers, add the meat and stir-fry it until it's almost cooked through, about 2 minutes. Transfer the meat to a plate. Add the remaining 1 tbsp vegetable oil, the ginger, and garlic to the hot pan and stir until fragrant, about 30 seconds. Add the carrots, green onions, and snow peas and continue to cook, tossing the vegetables around in the pan, until they're crisp-tender, about 2 minutes longer. The meat juices will cook onto the bottom of the pan, so if it threatens to burn, reduce the heat.

4. Return the meat to the pan and pour in the stir-fry sauce, tossing the veggies and meat for another minute or so and scraping up the browned bits from the pan bottom. The sauce will thicken as it heats up. Taste and season with more soy sauce or chili garlic sauce if you want the dish saltier or spicier.

5. Mound the cooked rice onto two warmed plates and top it with the meat and vegetables. Sprinkle with the cilantro and serve hot.

it's that easy: For the best-tasting zest, look for oranges with a dimpled surface instead of smooth skin, and choose the heaviest oranges in the bin for the most juice.

extra hungry? Instead of white rice, choose brown rice. It has more fiber, so it's more healthful and keeps you full for a longer period of time.

in the glass: An Oregon Pinot Noir from Firesteed has a lot of earthy red fruit to complement the orange and spice in this stir-fry.

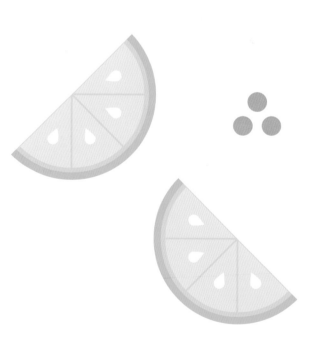

Sweet-and-Sour Stir-Fry

with BEEF, BROCCOLI, and MANGO

Eating out at the Chinese restaurant in our town was a real treat for me as a child. My mom always ordered the sweet-and-sour beef and everyone at the table would clamor for a taste. This version, though decidedly less ketchupy (sorry, Mom), has all the hallmarks of the original: a tart-sweet sauce enrobing crispy fresh vegetables and tender beef.

8 oz/225 g top sirloin,
thinly sliced into 3-in/7.5-cm strips

Salt and freshly ground black pepper

1/3 cup/75 ml chicken broth

2 tbsp ketchup

2 tbsp cider vinegar

2 tbsp soy sauce

2 tbsp sugar

2 tsp cornstarch

1 tsp chili garlic sauce,
plus more if needed

2 tbsp vegetable oil

1 small yellow onion, sliced

2 stalks broccoli, florets cut into
bite-size pieces, tender parts of the
stalks peeled and thinly sliced

1 red, yellow, or orange bell pepper,
seeded, deribbed, and thinly sliced

2 garlic cloves, minced

1 tbsp peeled and minced fresh ginger

1/2 mango, peeled and diced
(see "It's that easy")

Microwave steam-in-the-bag rice for serving

2 tbsp minced fresh cilantro

1. Sprinkle the beef with salt and pepper. In a medium bowl, stir together the chicken broth, ketchup, vinegar, soy sauce, sugar, cornstarch, and chili garlic sauce. Add the sirloin and stir to coat it with the sauce. Set aside at room temperature.

2. Heat a 12-in/30.5-cm skillet over medium-high heat and add the vegetable oil. When the oil shimmers, add the onion and broccoli stalks to the pan and stir-fry for 2 minutes. Add the bell pepper, broccoli florets, garlic, and ginger and stir-fry until the bell pepper and broccoli florets begin to soften, about 2 minutes. Add the meat, with its marinade, and the mango to the hot pan and stir-fry it until the meat is almost cooked through, about 2 minutes. The sauce will thicken. Cover and reduce the heat to low. Simmer the vegetables and meat until the vegetables are crisp-tender, about 3 minutes longer. Taste and adjust the seasoning. Add more chili garlic sauce for a hotter dish.

3. Mound the cooked rice onto two warmed plates, top it with the beef and vegetables, and garnish with the cilantro. Serve hot.

it's that easy: Fresh mangoes are easy to prepare once you're familiar with their architecture. They have a large, wide, flat pit, kind of like the shape of your hand when your fingers are pressed together. Look down at the top of the mango; you can see that it is wider at one end. The pit runs right down the middle of the length, so there is of course more flesh on each side at the fatter end. Starting from the top (thinner) end, cut down just off center so that the knife slides along the flat surface of the pit. Cut down the other side, then peel and dice the mango halves. Choose fruit that gives lightly when pressed. If all the mangoes are hard, place one in a paper bag with an apple at room temperature for a few days to ripen it up more quickly.

extra hungry? Add some thawed frozen edamame. The meaty fresh soybeans pack a protein punch that will fill you up and keep you that way all evening long.

in the glass: A jammy, fruity, Australian Shiraz would be delicious with this sweet-tart meal. Look for bottlings from Rosemount Estate or Wolf Blass for intense flavor, fruit, and spice.

Rib-Eye Steaks Florentine

with PARSNIP-and-POTATO GALETTES

Ahhhhhh . . . rib-eye, one of the lushest cuts of steak, thanks to the generous marbling that runs through a steer's juicy ribs. Add a crispy-on-the-outside potato cake perfumed with parsnip and thyme, a few shavings of Parmesan, a drizzle of olive oil, and a splash of lemon and you'll summon a taste of the fertile valleys of Tuscany. But only if you feel like reliving a scene from the movie *Stealing Beauty*. Yes, it's that good.

Two 8-oz/225-g boneless rib-eye steaks, (see "It's that easy") about ³/₄ in/2 cm thick

Salt and freshly ground black pepper

1 Yukon gold potato, peeled and grated

1 parsnip, peeled and grated

1 tbsp all-purpose flour

¹/₄ tsp dried thyme

2 tbsp extra-virgin olive oil, plus more for drizzling

6 oz/170 g baby spinach (I use the bagged variety so I don't have to wash it)

Pinch of freshly grated nutmeg

Parmesan shavings, preferably Parmigiano-Reggiano, for garnish

¹/₂ lemon

---

1. About 30 minutes before you plan to eat, transfer the steaks from the fridge to the kitchen counter. (This step removes the chill from the meat so that it cooks faster and more evenly, resulting in a juicier steak.) Pat them dry with paper towels and season with salt and pepper on both sides.

2. While the steaks warm up, combine the potato and parsnip in a medium bowl and add the flour, thyme, ¹/₄ tsp salt, and pepper to taste. Stir to mix well.

3. Heat a 12-in/30.5-cm skillet over medium-high heat and add 1 tbsp of the olive oil. When the oil shimmers, add the potato-parsnip mixture in two mounds, flattening them into galettes (or pancakes) about 5 in/12 cm wide. Using the back side of a fork, scrunch and press on the top and sides of the galettes to make them neat and compact. Don't try to move them until they've browned on the bottom and firmed up overall, about 3 minutes. Using a thin-bladed spatula, carefully flip them over and press lightly with the spatula to flatten and compress. Cook until browned on the second side and cooked through, about 3 minutes longer. Transfer the galettes to a warmed plate and keep them warm under aluminum foil or in a low oven while you cook the steaks.

4. Add the remaining 1 tbsp olive oil to the hot pan and return to medium-high heat. When the oil shimmers, add the seasoned steaks. They should sizzle and spit a little. Remember how you didn't bother the pancakes until they'd browned? Same thing here. Cook the steaks until a crust forms on the bottom, about 4 minutes. Flip the steaks and cook the other side for about 3 minutes longer for medium-rare meat, 4 minutes for medium. Transfer the meat to a warmed plate and let it rest while you cook the spinach.

5. There should be some oil left in the pan along with some cooked on steak juices and seasoning, which will effortlessly add flavor to the spinach. Add the spinach (it can be wet if you had to wash it) to the pan along with the nutmeg and cook it just until it's wilted, about 1 minute. Add a splash of water and scrape up the browned meat bits on the pan bottom if they haven't already incorporated into the spinach. Taste for seasoning and remove the pan from the heat.

6. Put a galette on each of two warmed plates and top them with the spinach and steak. If you feel like living like an Italian tonight—and who wouldn't—garnish the top of the steaks with the cheese shavings, a drizzle of olive oil, and a squeeze of lemon.

it's that easy: As the name suggests, a rib-eye is cut from the rib section of a steer (it may also be called a Delmonico). Meat from the rib section is tender and marbled with the fat that makes a steak juicy and flavorful. Nearby are the loin and top sirloin cuts, so this steak comes from a pretty good neighborhood. It usually appears in your grocer's case in boneless form and that's how you want it here.

extra hungry? Serve some ciabatta bread and a plate of extra-virgin olive oil sprinkled with sea salt alongside.

in the glass: If you're feeling flush, go for a Barolo here. They're comparable to a fine Cabernet and the best ones are round and lush . . . perfect with a steak. If the coffers are a little low, go for a red blend like claret, which often combines Cabernet, Merlot, Zinfandel, and some of the lesser-known blendable red grapes. They are often a good value. One of my faves is Newton, which is delicious and priced right.

Flat-Iron Steak

with GREEN BEANS, CHILI-HOISIN SAUCE, *and* SESAME SEEDS

When fresh and crisp, green beans are one of the best-tasting vegetables in the market. Especially when dressed up in a Chinese sauce of hoisin and sesame oil. Not only are these delicious beans something to get excited about, the flat-iron steak is destined to be your new favorite cut. Inexpensive and more tender than strip steak, flat-iron is from a part of the shoulder, so there's a lot of flavor and marbling. Cook it like you would any steak, hot and fast, for the best results.

One 12- to 14-oz/ 340- to 400-g
flat-iron steak

Salt and freshly ground black pepper

1 lb/455 g trimmed and
snapped green beans

1 tbsp hoisin sauce (see "It's that easy")

1 tbsp rice vinegar (see "It's that easy")

1 tbsp soy sauce (see "It's that easy")

2 tsp toasted sesame oil (see "It's that easy")

1 tsp chili garlic sauce (see "It's that easy")

2 tbsp olive oil

2 tsp white or black sesame seeds

1. About 30 minutes before you plan to cook, transfer the steak from the fridge to the kitchen counter. (This step removes the chill from the meat so that it cooks faster and more evenly, resulting in a juicier steak.) Pat it dry with paper towels and sprinkle with salt and pepper on both sides.

2. Fill a 12-in/30.5-cm skillet with water up to about 1 in/2.5 cm from the top. Cover and bring to a boil over high heat. Add 2 tsp salt and the green beans and cook until the beans are crisp-tender, about 5 minutes. Drain the beans in a colander

set in the sink and rinse them under cold running water to stop the cooking. Set aside.

3. While the beans are cooking, in a small bowl, stir together the hoisin sauce, rice vinegar, soy sauce, sesame oil, and chili garlic sauce. Set aside.

4. Put the empty skillet over medium-high heat and add the olive oil. When the oil shimmers, add the steak. Cook until nicely browned on the bottom, about 5 minutes. Try to resist moving it; it'll brown more quickly if you just let it do its business.

Flip it over with tongs and add the green beans to the pan, nestling them down into the sides of the pan so that they touch the bottom and heat up. Cook the steak for another 3 minutes, moving the beans around, and then drizzle in the hoisin mixture. The pan will sizzle. Cook the steak for 1 minute longer for medium-rare, or 2 minutes for medium. Reduce the heat if the bottom of the pan starts to burn, or add a splash of water. Remove from the heat and transfer the steak to a cutting board. Tent the steak with aluminum foil and let rest for 3 or 4 minutes to let the juices settle before carving. Cover the beans in the pan so they stay hot while the steak sits.

5. Carve the steak into thin slices. (See "It's that easy," page 91.) Arrange the slices on warmed plates and mound the green beans alongside. Spoon the pan sauce over the meat and beans (thin it with a little hot water, if needed) and sprinkle the sesame seeds over the top. Serve hot.

it's that easy: *Here are a few helpful notes on Chinese ingredients. Hoisin is like Chinese barbecue sauce and can be found with the rice vinegar, soy sauce, sesame oil, and chili garlic sauce in the international section of your grocery store. Rice vinegar is milder and not as acidic as regular vinegar. I generally use regular soy sauce and stay away from the "lite" versions. The toasted sesame oil has a nutty flavor and should be kept in the fridge after opening. Chili garlic sauce is hot, hot stuff, so use it with caution if you're sensitive to heat. It will keep for up to a year in your refrigerator after opening and is a great addition to soups, stews, stir-fries, or anything that needs a little kick.*

extra hungry? *A salad of romaine lettuce and grape tomatoes drizzled with balsamic and a glug of olive oil would hit all the right notes.*

in the glass: *I can't resist a spicy Syrah or Australian Shiraz with steak, and I love how there are so many great affordable bottles available. One of my faves is an Aussie label, Marquis Philips from McLaren Vale. It's widely distributed and a great deal.*

Flank Steak

with CHIMICHURRI and SUMMER SQUASH HASH

Chimichurri is Argentina's version of ketchup. This tart and spicy salsa of parsley, vinegar, onion, garlic, and hot red pepper flakes complements everything from juicy grilled steak to roasted vegetables. The summer squash hash is a tasty blend of diced potatoes, yellow squash, and peas, all cooked up in the pan's meaty juices. On a white plate, this colorful meal really sings. In your mouth . . . it's a symphony.

One 12-oz/340-g flank steak, at room temperature

1 tbsp Montreal steak seasoning or other spice mix for steak (see "It's that easy")

3 green onions, white and tender green parts, thinly sliced

1/2 cup/20 g minced fresh flat-leaf parsley

2 garlic cloves, minced

4 tbsp/60 ml olive oil, plus more if needed

2 tsp red wine vinegar

1/4 tsp red pepper flakes

Salt and freshly ground black pepper

2 new potatoes, scrubbed and cut into 1/4-in/6-mm dice

1 summer squash, about 8 in/20 cm long, quartered lengthwise and cut into 1/4-in/6-mm slices

1/2 cup/70 g frozen peas, thawed

1. Cut the steak into two portions (so it will cook faster) and rub it generously on all sides with the steak seasoning. Set aside at room temperature.

2. In a small bowl, combine about one-third of the green onions, all of the parsley, and half of the garlic and toss to mix. Add 2 tbsp of the olive oil, the vinegar, the red pepper flakes, a pinch of salt, and a few grinds of pepper and stir with a fork to mix well.

Taste and adjust the seasoning. The sauce should be tart, but if it's too vinegary for you, add a little more salt and olive oil. Set the chimichurri sauce aside.

3. Heat a 12-in/30.5-cm skillet over medium-high heat and add the remaining 2 tbsp olive oil. When the oil shimmers, arrange the steaks in the pan and cook, undisturbed, until nicely browned on the bottom, about 4 minutes. Turn and cook

continued

on the second side for about 3 minutes longer for medium-rare steak, or 4 minutes for medium. (This cut is usually about ¹/₂ in/12 mm thick. If your steak is thicker, it might need to cook a little longer.) Remove the pan from the heat, transfer the steaks to a plate, and tent with aluminum foil to keep warm.

4. Add the potatoes to the hot pan and sauté until they soften, about 3 minutes. Add the squash, the remaining green onions, and a sprinkle of salt and pepper and sauté until the all of vegetables are tender, about 4 minutes longer. Some of the steak flavor will come up from the browned bits on the bottom of the pan, so the vegetables will turn a little brown. It's important to keep things sizzling; you may need to add a little more oil to the pan. Stir in the remaining garlic and the peas. Taste and adjust the seasoning. Sauté for another minute or so to blend the flavors and warm the peas. Remove the pan from the heat.

5. Carve the steak into thin slices. (See "It's that easy," page 91.)

6. Divide the steak and veggie hash between two warmed plates and garnish with a dollop or two of the chimichurri. Serve hot.

it's that easy: A widely accepted explanation for the wonder that is Montreal steak seasoning is that it evolved from the dry rub used for preserving smoked meats in that town in the '40s. The rub itself is believed to be a spin on the traditional pickling spices used by Montreal's Eastern European Jewish population. You can get all that history along with tons of flavor in a convenient bottle in any well-stocked spice section at the market. But if you have a favorite dry rub for steak, feel free to substitute that here, or mix up your own Montreal spice; there are recipes aplenty online.

extra hungry? Toast up thin slices of ciabatta bread and drizzle with olive oil. Sprinkle some grated Parmesan over the tops and brown them under the broiler for about 1 minute.

in the glass: Nothing goes with flank steak like Zinfandel. Brazin Old Vine Zin is a great weeknight bottle.

Hungarian Beef Goulash

with PARPIKA *and* DUMPLINGS

Beef goulash . . . it even sounds warm and homey. Sure to warm up hungry tummies on cold evenings, this stew is especially nice because it's stocked with vegetables, flavored with sweet paprika, enriched with sour cream, and topped with dumplings that would make your grandmother cry happy tears.

1 tbsp olive oil

2 slices bacon, chopped

12 oz/340 g top sirloin or flat-iron steak, trimmed and cut into 1-in/ 2.5-cm cubes

Salt

1 small yellow onion, cut into ½-in/12-mm dice

1 red bell pepper, seeded, deribbed, and cut into ½-in/12-mm dice

1 garlic clove, minced

1 tbsp sweet paprika, preferably Hungarian

1 tbsp tomato paste

3 new potatoes, scrubbed and cut into ½-in/12-mm dice

2 cups/480 ml beef broth

2 tbsp red wine vinegar

Freshly ground black pepper

½ cup/65 g all-purpose flour

½ tsp baking powder

¼ cup/60 ml milk

1 tbsp unsalted butter

¼ cup/55 g sour cream

1. Heat a 12-in/30.5-cm skillet over medium-high heat and add the olive oil. When the oil shimmers, add the bacon and cook, stirring, until it has given off its fat but isn't crispy yet, about 2 minutes. Add the beef and ½ tsp salt and spread the beef cubes out in an even layer in the pan. Let the meat brown on one side without moving it, about 3 minutes. Turn the meat with tongs or a fork to brown on a second side, another 2 minutes. Add the onion, bell pepper, garlic, paprika, and tomato paste and continue to sauté until the vegetables begin to soften and the bottom of the pan gets nice and brown, about

continued

99

4 minutes longer. Add the potatoes, beef broth, vinegar, and a few grinds of pepper and scrape up all the browned bits from the bottom of the pan. Bring the mixture to a simmer.

2. Meanwhile, in a bowl, whisk together the flour, baking powder, and 1/4 tsp salt. Combine the milk and butter in a cup and microwave on high for 10 seconds at a time until the butter is melted. Add the milk mixture to the flour mixture and stir just until combined. Drop the batter by tablespoonfuls into the simmering stew; you should have enough for about about eight dumplings.

3. Cover the skillet, reduce the heat to low, and simmer the stew until the vegetables and dumplings are tender, about 15 minutes. (Don't peek! The steam will be released and your dumplings may not be as puffy and light as they could be.) To check for doneness, run a toothpick into a dumpling. It should come out with dry crumbs adhering to it, not wet and gooey. If it's wet, cover and cook another 3 minutes and check again.

4. Scoop the dumplings into warmed bowls. Taste the stew for seasoning, adding more salt or pepper if needed. Ladle the stew over the dumplings and top each portion with a dollop of the sour cream. Serve hot.

it's that easy: I direct you to brown the meat and then add vegetables, paprika, and tomato paste, and cook until it all browns on the bottom of the pan. Don't stress over what might seem like a sticky pan; the browned bits will all come up when you add the broth, and the flavor of the stew will be the richer for it.

extra hungry? For a lovely salad to pair with this stew, peel, seed, and thinly slice a cucumber and blend it with 1 to 2 tbsp sour cream, a splash of white wine vinegar, and season with salt and pepper.

in the glass: Every now and then a Merlot is the right wine for a dish—and this is one of those times. Look for bottlings by Rutherford, Simi, Clos du Bois, and Round Hill, all enjoyable quaffs.

Veal Rolls

with CURRANTS, PINE NUTS, *and* PARMESAN POLENTA STACKS

Little veal rolls stuffed with currants, parsley, Parmesan cheese, pine nuts, and bread crumbs are almost too delicious to make for Wednesday night. They shout, "It's time to party and have fun!" I love the textures in this meal, from the stuffing with a mix of crunch and creamy to the polenta rounds with their soft insides and crunchy fried exteriors. Maybe it's too early in the week to party, but at the very least, you can have a party in your mouth.

2 tbsp currants

2 tbsp chopped fresh flat-leaf parsley, plus 1 tsp

1/2 cup/60 g freshly grated Parmesan cheese

3 tbsp panko bread crumbs

2 tbsp pine nuts

4 veal scallops (cutlets), about 3 oz/ 85 g each, pounded even thinner (see "It's that easy," page 105)

Salt and freshly ground black pepper

2 tbsp olive oil

Eight 1/2-in/12-mm slices precooked, ready-to-heat polenta (see "It's that easy")

1 shallot, minced

1/3 cup/75 ml dry white wine

1 tbsp unsalted butter

1. Preheat the oven to 375°F/190°C/gas 5. In a small bowl, combine the currants with hot water to cover and let stand for 5 minutes.

2. Scoop up 1 tbsp of the currant-soaking liquid and transfer it to a medium bowl. Drain the currants and add them to the bowl along with the 2 tbsp

parsley, 1/4 cup/30 g of the Parmesan, the panko, and pine nuts. Mix the ingredients with a fork until evenly moistened.

3. Lay the veal on the work surface and sprinkle with salt and pepper. Spoon equal amounts of the stuffing down the length of the veal strips. Spread

continued

in a thin layer, leaving a border of about 1/2 in/ 12 mm around the edges uncovered. Starting at a narrow end, gently roll up each into a tight cylinder. Secure the rolls with toothpicks.

4. Heat a 12-in/30.5-cm ovenproof skillet over medium-high heat and add 1 tbsp of the olive oil. When it shimmers, add the polenta rounds and cook until browned and crispy on the bottom, about 3 minutes. Carefully flip them over with a thin-edged spatula and cook until browned on the second side, another 2 minutes or so. Sprinkle the remaining 1/4 cup/30 g Parmesan on four of the rounds, dividing it evenly, and then top them with the uncheesed rounds. The cheese should melt and act as a kind of glue to hold the polenta stacks together. Transfer to a plate and cover to keep warm.

5. Scrape up any polenta scraps in the pan with the spatula and discard them (or nibble them up). Add the remaining 1 tbsp olive oil to the hot pan and add the veal rolls. Cook, turning as needed, until golden on all sides, about 4 minutes total. Return the polenta rounds to the pan and transfer to the oven to reheat the polenta and finish cooking the veal, about 8 minutes.

6. Remove the pan from the oven (be careful, the handle will be blazing hot) and transfer the rolls and polenta rounds to two warmed plates. Cover to keep warm. Carefully return the pan to medium-high heat and add the shallot to the pan juices, stirring until softened, about 1 minute. Add the wine and cook, scraping up any browned bits from the bottom of the pan, until the liquid is reduced by half, about 2 minutes. Remove the pan from the heat and add

the butter, swirling the pan to melt it. Drizzle the wine sauce over the veal rolls, garnish the plates with the 1 tsp parsley, and serve hot.

it's that easy: Ready-to-heat prepared polenta is a weeknight cook's godsend, because it tastes almost as fresh as if you just cooked it, and there are so many ways to use it. Cooked polenta is packaged in "logs" of about 1 lb/455 g. After you slice off the polenta rounds for this recipe, you have infinite options for how to use up the rest of the log in the next few days—for example, as the crust for a frittata or smothered with tomato sauce for a vegetarian main course, or just fry it up and serve with maple syrup for an easy, breakfast-y dinner.

extra hungry? A few handfuls of arugula tossed with a squirt of lemon, a glug of olive oil, and a scattering of rinsed capers would be a nice counterpoint to the richness of this dish.

in the glass: For a "good enough for company" meal like this, I'd like to uncork a Pouilly-Fuissé from Jadot. Made in the Burgundy region of France from Chardonnay grapes, it's light, refreshing, and can be found inexpensively almost anywhere.

Lamb Kebabs

with HARISSA, CHICKPEAS, *and* SUMMER SQUASH

Everyday kebabs of pork, beef, or chicken are certainly delicious, but there's something celebratory about lamb kebabs, especially when the meat has a short bath in the flavors of North Africa: spicy harissa paste, garlic, and olive oil. A quick sauté of onion, summer squash, and chickpeas flavored with the marinade you used for the lamb makes this dish easy enough for weeknights but good enough for company. And a drizzle of lemony sour cream takes this meal from really good to really, really good. After all, we are celebrating these lamb kebabs, right?

1 garlic clove, minced

*2 tbsp harissa paste
(see "It's that easy")*

2 tbsp olive oil

*12 oz/340 g boneless lamb sirloin or loin
roast, cut into 1-in/2.5-cm cubes*

Salt and freshly ground black pepper

1 small yellow onion, diced

*2 summer squash, halved lengthwise and
cut crosswise into slices about ½ in/12 mm thick*

One 15-oz/430-g can chickpeas, drained

¼ cup/55 g sour cream

Juice from ½ lemon

2 tsp minced fresh cilantro

1. Soak four 6-in/15-cm wooden skewers in water for about 10 minutes.

2. In a medium bowl, combine the garlic, harissa, and 1 tbsp of the olive oil. Set aside about 1 tbsp of the mixture. Add the lamb to the bowl and toss to coat it with the spice paste. Thread the lamb loosely onto the soaked skewers and sprinkle them with salt and pepper. Let the lamb sit at room temperature for 15 to 20 minutes.

3. Preheat the broiler with the rack in the second position from the top.

4. Heat a 12-in/30.5-cm ovenproof skillet over medium-high heat and add the remaining 1 tbsp olive oil. When the oil shimmers, add the lamb skewers and brown them on one side, about 1 minute. Turn the lamb and brown the opposite side for another minute. Remove the pan from the heat and

continued

HUNGRY FOR MORE

transfer the kebabs to a plate. (They will not be cooked through at this point.)

5. Return the pan to medium-high heat and add the onion, 1/4 tsp salt, and a few grinds of pepper. Sauté the onion until it begins to soften, about 2 minutes, then add the squash. Continue to sauté until the squash begins to soften, another 2 minutes or so, and then add the chickpeas, another sprinkle of salt and pepper, and the reserved 1 tbsp harissa blend. Toss the vegetables with the spices and cook until heated through and tender, about 3 minutes longer. Lay the kebabs on top of the veggies and slip the pan under the broiler for 3 minutes to cook the kebabs to medium-rare, or 4 minutes for medium. Meanwhile, in a bowl, stir together the sour cream and lemon juice.

6. Mound the chickpeas and vegetables onto two warmed plates and top them with the kebabs, a drizzle of the lemon sour cream, and a sprinkling of the cilantro. Serve hot.

it's that easy: *Harissa is a fiery Tunisian spice paste made from hot chiles, lemon, garlic, and ground spices like cumin and coriander. Sort of like the ketchup of North Africa, harissa can be rubbed onto lamb, goat, fish, and vegetables, or served as a condiment to ramp up the flavor of couscous-based dishes. At my grocery, it comes in a small metal can. Once opened, just transfer the paste to an airtight container and pour a little olive oil over the top to help keep it from drying out. Tightly sealed, it will last for months and months in the fridge (maybe even years), but use it up by putting a dollop on your next frittata, in ho-hum barbecue sauce, or just about anyplace you'd like a little "pow!"*

extra hungry? *Add 1 cup/140 g thawed frozen green beans along with the chickpeas. They add a nice touch of green and are delicious with the flavors here as well.*

in the glass: *A spicy meal like this is looking for a spicy wine. Try a full-bodied old-vine Zinfandel from Lodi, California, such as Klinker Brick. Lodi is home to many vines that are more than fifty years old; these are thought to yield a more concentrated fruit, adding more body, balance, and structure to the wine. If the grapes are from Lodi, most of the labels will say so. Check it out.*

Lamb Korma

How about a trip to India tonight? Redolent with cinnamon, coriander, cardamom, and ginger, korma is a fragrant Indian dish more often reserved for time-consuming celebratory-event cooking than for dinner on a hungry Tuesday night. I've simplified it without sacrificing flavor by using a tender cut of meat and the spice blend garam masala instead of the multitude of traditional spices. It's so rich and delicious, you'll think it's been simmering for hours, and the addition of yogurt makes it deliciously creamy without the calories.

1 tsp garam masala (see "It's that easy"), plus more if needed

Pinch of ground cloves

Pinch of cayenne pepper

Pinch of ground cinnamon

Salt and freshly ground black pepper

10 oz/280 g boneless lamb sirloin or loin roast, cut into 1-in/2.5-cm cubes

1 tbsp unsalted butter

1 small yellow onion, thinly sliced

1 tbsp peeled and minced fresh ginger

1 garlic clove, minced

1/2 cup/120 ml beef broth

1/2 cup/70 g frozen peas, thawed

1/2 cup/115 g whole-fat plain Greek yogurt

Microwave steam-in-the-bag rice for serving

1/4 cup/35 g slivered almonds

2 tsp minced fresh cilantro

1. In a medium bowl, combine the garam masala, cloves, cayenne, cinnamon, 1/2 tsp salt, and a few grinds of black pepper. Add the lamb and toss to coat with the spices.

2. In a 12-in/30.5-cm skillet over medium-high heat, melt the butter. Add the onion and sauté until softened, about 1 minute. Add the ginger,

garlic, and lamb and cook until the lamb is browned on the first side, 2 to 3 minutes. Turn the lamb to brown the opposite side, another 2 minutes or so. Add the beef broth and scrape up the browned bits on the bottom of the pan. Bring to a simmer, cover, and reduce the heat to low. Simmer the korma until the lamb is tender and the flavors have blended, about 15 minutes. Remove the pan from the heat and stir in the peas. Let the korma cool for a few minutes so that the yogurt doesn't curdle, then add the yogurt and stir until well blended. Taste and add more garam masala, salt, and/or pepper if you like.

3. Spoon the cooked rice onto two warmed plates and top it with the lamb korma. Sprinkle the tops with the almonds and cilantro and serve hot.

it's that easy: Garam masala is an Indian spice blend of coriander, cumin, cinnamon, clove, cardamom, cay-enne, and even spices that don't begin with a C, such as fennel, mace, and nutmeg. Buy it at the grocery store or online. It's also delicious sprinkled over chicken, fish, or vegetable dishes.

extra hungry? For your own version of an Indian raita, slice up tomato, cucumber, and a little red onion and toss them with a splash of cider vinegar; a glug of olive oil; salt, black pepper, and red pepper flakes to taste; and a dollop of yogurt.

in the glass: Look for a Pinot Noir from New Zealand. Babich makes a nice bottle brimming with red berry fruit and spice.

POULTRY WITH SOUL

CHAPTER

3

egg, turkey & chicken dinners

Fluffy Spring Frittata

with ASPARAGUS, BELL PEPPERS, *and* GRUYÈRE

This frittata is special because of all the lovely green asparagus, chunks of sweet red pepper, and tender potato, making this dish a perfect springtime dinner option. My take on the frittata: lots of veggies on the inside with just enough egg to bind it all together. And cheese, of course. We couldn't forget the cheese.

6 large eggs

2 tbsp milk or water

Salt and freshly ground black pepper

Pinch of freshly grated nutmeg

Pinch of cayenne pepper

2 tbsp unsalted butter

1 small yellow onion, finely diced

3 new potatoes, scrubbed and cut into 1/4-in/6-mm dice

1 red bell pepper, seeded, deribbed, and cut into 1/4-in/6-mm dice

1 bunch asparagus, tough woody ends snapped off (see "It's that easy"), cut into 1-in/2.5-cm pieces

6 oz/170 g Gruyère cheese, shredded

1. Preheat the broiler with the rack in the second position from the top.

2. In a medium bowl, whisk together the eggs, milk, 1/2 tsp salt, a few grinds of pepper, the nutmeg, and cayenne.

3. In a 12-in/30.5-cm ovenproof skillet over medium-high heat, melt the butter. When the butter is melted and sizzles, add the onion and potatoes and a sprinkle of salt and pepper. Cook, stirring every now and then, until the potatoes

begin to soften, about 4 minutes. Add the bell pepper and asparagus and another sprinkle of salt and pepper and continue to cook and stir occasionally until the vegetables are tender and the potatoes are lightly browned, another 4 minutes or so. Taste a piece of asparagus to see if it's tender. If it's not, cook it another minute or two. Spread the vegetables evenly over the bottom of the pan and sprinkle the cheese over the top.

4. Pour the eggs evenly over the vegetables in the pan and reduce the heat to low. Cover the pan and cook for 2 minutes, then remove the lid and transfer the pan to the broiler. Broil the frittata until the top is lightly browned and the eggs have firmed up in the center, about 4 minutes. To test, press the center of the frittata lightly with your finger. If it feels firm, it's done.

5. Remove the frittata from the oven and let it rest for 3 minutes on a wire rack on the countertop to continue to firm up before cutting it into wedges. It will be puffy when it comes out of the oven but will deflate and become firmer as it cools. Serve the frittata hot or at room temperature.

it's that easy: The cut ends of asparagus are tough and should be trimmed before cooking. The easy way is to cut the tough ends while the bunch is still wrapped in the rubber bands. Just rinse the asparagus bundle and cut away the lower 3 in/7.5 cm with a sharp knife, then proceed to slice the asparagus down as directed.

extra hungry? Add a loaf of crusty bread with extra-virgin olive oil for dipping. I like to sprinkle the oil with French gray sea salt. With each bite of oil-dipped bread, the little sodium crystals explode in your mouth. If you don't have any gray salt, kosher will do.

in the glass: A frittata is one of our favorite dinners, especially when paired with a glass of Prosecco, a slightly fizzy white wine from Northern Italy. I get excited just thinking about it.

Winter Frittata

with ESCAROLE, BACON, *and* FETA CHEESE

The frittata has been relegated to the breakfast and lunch scene for too long. It's one of the easiest, fastest, and most filling meals going. The secret to making a frittata a complete meal is to fill it up with lots of great-tasting vegetables. Whatever floats your boat—just load the pan with veggies and cook them until tender. This one is full of greens, bacon, and salty feta cheese. It just might be my favorite. We sometimes have a slice of frittata left over. Just refrigerate it until the next day and have it for lunch.

6 large eggs

2 tbsp milk or water

Salt and freshly ground black pepper

Pinch of freshly grated nutmeg

4 slices bacon

1 small yellow onion, thinly sliced

1 tbsp olive oil (optional)

3 new potatoes, scrubbed and cut into 1/4-in/6-mm dice

4 or 5 handfuls washed and torn escarole or other bitter leafy greens (see "It's that easy")

1 garlic clove, minced

1/2 cup/70 g crumbled feta cheese

1. Preheat the broiler with the rack in the second position from the top.

2. In a medium bowl, whisk together the eggs, milk, 1/2 tsp salt, a few grinds of pepper, and the nutmeg.

3. Heat a 12-in/30.5-cm ovenproof skillet over medium-high heat and add the bacon. Cook, turning as needed, until browned and crispy on both sides, 5 to 7 minutes total. Transfer to paper towels to drain. When it's cool, crumble the bacon and set aside.

4. Add the onion to the hot bacon fat in the pan and sauté until it softens, about 2 minutes. If there isn't enough fat in the pan, go ahead and add the olive oil. Add the potatoes and a sprinkle of salt and pepper and sauté, stirring every now and then, until

continued

POULTRY WITH SOUL

121

the potatoes are tender, about 4 minutes. Add the escarole by the handful and cook until it wilts, adding more handfuls as there is room in the pan. Add the garlic and another sprinkle of salt and pepper and cook until the escarole is tender, about 2 minutes longer.

5. Spread the filling evenly over the bottom of the pan and scatter the crumbled bacon and feta over the top. Pour the eggs evenly over the vegetables and reduce the heat to low. Cover the pan and cook for 2 minutes, then remove the lid and transfer the pan to the broiler. Broil the frittata until the top is lightly browned and the eggs have firmed up in the center, about 4 minutes. To test, press the center of the frittata lightly with your finger. If it feels firm, it's done.

6. Remove the frittata from the oven and let it rest for 3 minutes on a wire rack on the countertop to continue to firm up before cutting it into wedges. It will be puffy when it comes out of the oven but will deflate and become firmer as it cools. Serve the frittata hot or at room temperature.

it's that easy: This frittata is a great way to clean out your crisper drawer. Throw in any bits of leftover greens, like radicchio, romaine lettuce, or arugula. A blend always tastes best.

extra hungry? Add a refreshing salad of romaine lettuce, diced oranges, olives, and thinly sliced fennel with a splash of white wine vinegar and a glug of olive oil.

in the glass: A Sauvignon Blanc like Cloudy Bay from New Zealand would be delicious with this simple meal, as would a glass of New Zealand Pinot Noir if you're in the mood for a red. Look for Delta Vineyard Pinot Noir or Crossroads Destination Series for great bottles at low prices.

Wild Mushroom Frittata

with CHEDDAR, GREEN ONIONS, *and* PEAS

The beauty of a frittata is that it can be filled with just about anything, but the wild mushrooms in this one are especially delicious when combined with fluffy eggs and Cheddar cheese. To fill up the middle, I added green onions, peas, potatoes, and fresh thyme. It's actually easier to make this frittata than to go out to eat. Such a beautiful thing.

6 large eggs

2 tbsp milk or water

Salt and freshly ground black pepper

Pinch of freshly grated nutmeg

Pinch of cayenne pepper

2 tbsp unsalted butter

3 new potatoes, scrubbed and cut into 1/4-in/6-mm dice

4 green onions, white and tender green parts, thinly sliced

10 oz/280 g mixed wild mushrooms (see "It's that easy"), such as cremini, shiitake, and oyster, brushed clean and sliced

1 garlic clove, minced

1 tsp minced fresh thyme

1/2 cup/70 g frozen peas, thawed

1/2 cup/55 g shredded Cheddar cheese

1. Preheat the broiler with the rack in the second position from the top.

2. In a medium bowl, whisk together the eggs, milk, 1/2 tsp salt, a few grinds of pepper, the nutmeg, and cayenne.

3. In a 12-in/30.5-cm ovenproof skillet over medium-high heat, melt the butter. When the butter is melted and hot, add the potatoes and a sprinkle of salt and pepper. Cook the potatoes, stirring every now and then, until they begin to soften, about 3 minutes. Add the green onions, mushrooms, garlic, thyme, and another sprinkle of salt and pepper and continue to cook and stir until the mushrooms have given off their liquid and are dry, about 4 minutes. Add the peas and cook until all of the veggies are tender and the peas are warmed through, another minute or two. Taste and adjust the seasoning. Spread the filling evenly over the bottom of the pan and sprinkle the cheese over the top.

continued

123

4. Pour the eggs evenly over the vegetables in the pan and reduce the heat to low. Cover the pan and cook for 2 minutes, then remove the lid and transfer the pan to the broiler. Broil the frittata until the top is lightly browned and the eggs have firmed up in the center, about 4 minutes. To test, press the center of the frittata lightly with your finger. If it feels firm, it's done.

5. Remove the frittata from the oven and let it rest for 3 minutes on a wire rack on the countertop to continue to firm up before cutting it into wedges. It will be puffy when it comes out of the oven but will deflate and become firmer as it cools. Serve the frittata hot or at room temperature.

it's that easy: This makes an über-savory dinner for two . . . especially if you use wild mushrooms, which are more flavorful. No need to break the bank on chanterelles here; just use whatever looks good at the grocery. I avoid the mushrooms packaged in plastic, as they have a tendency to become slimy. Buy them from the open bins where you can pick and choose the best ones.

extra hungry? How about a mug of that old standby Campbell's Tomato Soup? Umm, umm good.

in the glass: The earthy nature of the mushrooms will make a Beaujolais a nice partner to this dish. The easiest-to-find Beaujolais seems to come from Duboeuf and Jadot. Lucky for us, they are tasty bottles for the price.

Turkey Tonkatsu

with CABBAGE, PORTOBELLOS, *and* PICKLED GINGER

Tonkatsu is a popular Japanese dish of breaded and deep-fried cutlet—kind of a Japanese schnitzel, if you will. A dip into mustard-flavored egg and extra-flaky panko bread crumbs and a quick sauté in sizzling hot pan renders the turkey crispy, tender, and full of flavor. Traditionally served with raw cabbage and pickled vegetables, this version of *tonkatsu* includes sautéed portobello mushrooms and napa cabbage laced with soy and pickled ginger . . . just enough to keep the Japanese theme but with an adjustment for Western tastes.

½ lb/225 g turkey cutlets

Salt and freshly ground black pepper

1 large egg

1 tbsp Dijon mustard

1 tbsp water

1 cup/110 g panko bread crumbs

3 tbsp vegetable oil

3 cups/255 g thinly sliced napa or savoy cabbage

1 small yellow onion, thinly sliced

2 large portobello mushroom caps, feathery gills scraped out with a teaspoon and discarded

1 tbsp soy sauce

2 tbsp pickled ginger (see "It's that easy")

1. Working with one at a time, place the turkey cutlets between sheets of plastic wrap or wax paper and, using the flat side of a meat pounder or a small, heavy skillet, pound to a thickness of about ⅛ in/ 3 mm. Sprinkle the turkey all over with salt and pepper and set aside.

2. Whisk the egg, mustard, and water together in a shallow bowl. Spread the panko on a large plate.

Dip a turkey cutlet in the egg, then dredge in the panko, covering both sides completely. Lay the cutlet on a plate. Repeat to coat the remaining cutlets.

3. Heat a 12-in/30.5-cm skillet over medium-high heat and add 2 tbsp of the vegetable oil. When the oil shimmers, add half the turkey cutlets and cook until browned on the first side, about 3 minutes. Don't move them while they brown, and don't try to turn them if they are stuck to the pan; they will release when they are sufficiently crisp and brown. Give them a nudge to check for sticking and when they release, turn them over with tongs and brown on the other side, about 2 minutes. Transfer the cutlets to two warmed plates and cover to keep them warm (or place in a low oven). Repeat the process with the remaining cutlets.

4. Add the remaining 1 tbsp oil to the hot pan. Add the cabbage and onion and stir to coat with the oil. Move the cabbage mixture to one side of the pan and add the mushrooms to the empty half, top-sides down. Cook the mushroom caps until browned on the first side, about 2 minutes, meanwhile stirring the cabbage mixture occasionally. Turn the mushrooms over and brown the other side, another 2 minutes or so. Continue to stir the cabbage every now and then. Drizzle the soy sauce over the cabbage and mushrooms along with a few grinds of pepper and toss to combine well. Remove the pan from the heat, cover tightly, and let stand for the mushrooms to continue to soften and become tender, about 2 minutes. Transfer the mushrooms to the plates with the turkey cutlets and top them with the seasoned cabbage. Scatter the pickled ginger over the top of everything and serve right away.

it's that easy: You can find pickled ginger in a jar in the refrigerated section at your market. We tend to think of it as a partner with sushi, but it is a terrific condiment for grilled meats and vegetables, or anything that needs a bit of Asian mojo. At my market they also sell it packaged in smaller containers near the sushi. Feel free to pick up a container of wasabi as well if you want to give this dish some serious heat.

extra hungry? A little color would be welcome on the plate. Microwave some frozen edamame and blend them into the cabbage for some good green stuff.

in the glass: Look for a rich and fruity white like Pinot Grigio to accompany this dish. There are countless inexpensive bottlings from Italy, such as Marco Felluga, and more and more of this popular wine originates in California and the Pacific Northwest as well. Explore.

Balsamic Turkey

with ARTICHOKES and EGGPLANT CAPONATA

Caponata is a Sicilian vegetable dish containing eggplant, capers, olives, garlic, and onion. Traditionally, caponata is served as a dip, but it also makes a delicious side dish. The addition of vinegar, raisins, and honey makes it sweet and tart as well as earthy and salty—there's just a whole lot of flavor going on. The balsamic-glazed turkey cutlet in this recipe is topped with marinated artichoke hearts and Parmesan cheese, and may well remind you of that cheesy artichoke dip your mom used to make for card club. But in a good way, I promise.

10 oz/280 g turkey cutlets

Salt and freshly ground black pepper

2 tbsp olive oil, plus more if needed

1 Italian eggplant, cut into ½-in/12-mm dice

1 small red bell pepper, seeded, deribbed, and cut into ½-in/12-mm dice

1 small yellow onion, finely diced

1 celery stalk, finely diced

2 garlic cloves, minced

6 large green olives, pitted and chopped

4 tbsp/60 ml balsamic vinegar, plus more if needed

2 tbsp golden raisins

1 tbsp honey

2 tsp capers, rinsed well and patted dry (see "It's that easy")

6 oz/170 g marinated artichoke hearts, drained and chopped

⅓ cup/40 g freshly grated Parmesan cheese

1 tbsp minced fresh flat-leaf parsley

1. Preheat the broiler with the rack in the second position from the top.

2. Pat the turkey dry and sprinkle all over with salt and pepper.

3. Heat a 12-in/30.5-cm ovenproof skillet over medium-high heat and add the olive oil. When the oil shimmers, add the eggplant, bell pepper, onion, celery, ½ tsp salt, and a few grinds of pepper. Sauté until the vegetables are almost tender and beginning to brown, about 6 minutes. The eggplant will absorb most of the oil in the pan; add more oil if you think it needs it. Add the garlic, olives, 3 tbsp of the vinegar, the raisins, honey, and capers and stir it up well to blend the flavors. The caponata will sizzle lots. Reduce the heat if the bottom of the pan threatens to scorch. Stir until the vegetables are tender and mushy, another 3 minutes or so. The liquid should be evaporated. Taste and adjust the seasoning with more salt, pepper, or vinegar. Remove the pan from the heat.

4. Brush the turkey on both sides with the remaining 1 tbsp balsamic and lay it on top of the caponata. Slip the pan under the broiler and broil until the turkey is almost cooked through, about 3 minutes. Meanwhile, in a bowl, stir together the artichokes and Parmesan. Remove the pan from the oven and top the turkey with the artichoke mixture. Return the pan to the broiler and broil until the turkey is cooked through and the topping is hot and melted, about 3 minutes longer. Remove the pan from the oven and sprinkle the parsley over the dish. Transfer the turkey cutlets to two warmed plates, scoop the caponata on the side, and serve hot.

variation: Thinly sliced pork chop cutlets are a delicious stand-in for the turkey as well.

it's that easy: Capers come either packed in brine or dry-coated with salt. You can use the brined ones straight from the jar, but the salt-packed ones need a good rinse to wash the salt away.

extra hungry? Add a few slices of freshly baked focaccia from your local bakery.

in the glass: A medium-bodied Syrah has what it takes to make this dish sing. Look for bottlings from Terlato or Peter Lehmann for good taste and value.

Chicken Stew

with TOMATOES, ORANGES, and OLIVES

You know how good a soft cashmere scarf feels around your neck on a blustery day? Think of this dish as a cashmere scarf for your taste buds. The leek really adds a subtle flavor as only a leek will, so try to use it if you can. If finding a leek is too much trouble, go ahead and use a small onion, thinly sliced. Carrot and celery round out the veggies in the stew, with orange juice and diced tomatoes tarting up the whole thing. The olives add a briny touch and the orange zest gives this chicken-in-a-pot a bright citrusy note that you'll find particularly addictive. Kind of like that cashmere scarf.

6 boneless, skinless chicken thighs (see "It's that easy")

Salt and freshly ground black pepper

2 tbsp olive oil

1 leek, white and tender green parts, trimmed, rinsed thoroughly, and thinly sliced (see "It's that easy," page 33)

1 carrot, peeled and thinly sliced

1 celery stalk, thinly sliced

1/2 tsp dried thyme

2 garlic cloves, minced

Juice of 2 oranges, plus zest of 1 orange

One 14 1/2-oz/415-g can diced tomatoes, with juices

1/3 cup/55 g mixed Kalamata and green olives, pitted and halved

2 tbsp minced fresh flat-leaf parsley

Microwave steam-in-the-bag rice for serving

1. Pat the chicken dry and sprinkle all over with salt and pepper.

2. Heat a 12-in/30.5-cm skillet over medium-high heat and add the olive oil. When the oil shimmers, add the leek, carrot, celery, thyme, and 1/4 tsp salt and sauté until the vegetables soften, about 3 minutes. Add the chicken and continue to cook until the bottom of the pan has turned a rich brown, about 4 minutes longer. Add the garlic, orange juice, and tomatoes with their juices and bring to a simmer, stirring to scrape up the browned bits from the

continued

bottom of the pan. Reduce the heat to low, cover, and simmer the stew until the chicken is tender and shreds easily, about 30 minutes.

3. Using a slotted spoon or tongs, transfer the chicken thighs to a large plate and let cool slightly. When it's cool enough to handle, cut or shred the meat into bite-size pieces. Return the chicken to the pot and add the olives, half of the parsley, and half of the orange zest. Taste and season the stew with more salt and pepper if it needs it.

4. Scoop the cooked rice into two warmed shallow bowls and top with the chicken stew. Sprinkle with the remaining parsley and zest and serve hot.

it's that easy: *Stews and braises are all about the sauce, and when it comes to creating a sauce rich with chicken flavor, chicken thighs reign supreme. Don't even think about trying to make this dish with chicken breasts. They're too lean and don't have enough flavor to share with the surrounding liquid.*

extra hungry? *Olive oil–toasted bread is so easy: just drizzle slices of nice crusty bread with olive oil and toast in your toaster for a quick fix.*

in the glass: *A Châteauneuf-du-Pape would be perfect with this zesty chicken stew. Look for a bottle from Joseph Drouhin for a good value, but if you feel like a splurge, try a bottle of Télégramme. It's the second bottling from the venerable Vieux Télégraphe label and so has a lower price tag, but with much of the charm of its more expensive sibling.*

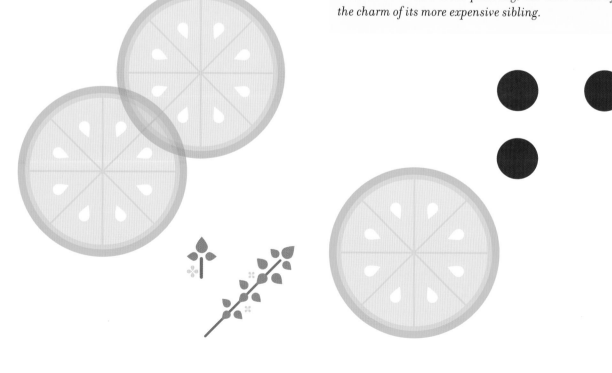

Cornflake-Crusted Chicken Fingers

with ROSEMARY–SWEET POTATO PAN FRIES and CHUTNEY DIPPING SAUCE

It may have a bit of an image problem, but I give a big thumbs-up to the crispy chicken finger. I don't like to use those overpriced tenders with that pesky tendon that runs through the length; cutting your own from a good-quality breast is easy, and highlights the virtues of America's favorite white meat. Quick-cooking slices dredged in crispy cornflake crumbs (conveniently, you can now buy prepared crumbs in boxes), my crunchy chicken digits are accompanied by a dipping sauce of Major Grey's chutney spiked with mayo and mustard.

2 tbsp Dijon mustard

2 tbsp mayonnaise

Salt and freshly ground black pepper

2 boneless, skinless chicken breast halves, each cut crosswise on the diagonal into 6 slices

1/2 cup/55 g cornflake crumbs (a box of prepared crumbs saves time)

2 medium or 1 large sweet potato, peeled and cut into sticks about 6 in/15 cm long and no more than 1/2 in/12 mm wide (see "It's that easy")

2 tsp olive oil, plus 3 tbsp, or more if needed

Leaves of 1 sprig fresh rosemary, minced

1/4 cup/55 g of your favorite chutney from a jar

1. In a large bowl, combine 1 tbsp of the mustard, 1 tbsp of the mayonnaise, 1/4 tsp salt, and a few grinds of pepper and stir to mix. Add the chicken and toss to coat evenly. Pour the cornflake crumbs onto a plate and dredge the chicken in the crumbs, pressing to coat each piece completely. Spread them on a plate to dry slightly while you cook the potatoes.

continued

POULTRY WITH SOUL

135

2. In a bowl or right on the cutting board you used for cutting the fries, drizzle the potatoes with the 2 tsp olive oil and toss them with the rosemary and a generous sprinkling of salt and pepper.

3. Heat a 12-in/30.5-cm skillet over medium-high heat and add 2 tbsp of the olive oil. Quickly add the sweet potatoes on their biggest flat side in a single layer. You may need to do this in two batches; do not crowd the pan. The fries will spit, so use a splatter screen if you have one. Don't move them. Just let them brown on that side for about 4 minutes, checking the underside of a fry occasionally to be sure that they don't overbrown or burn. Depending on your stove, you may have to adjust the heat up or down. Turn the fries with tongs or a fork and cook until browned on the opposite side, 3 or 4 minutes longer. The sugar in the potatoes will make them very brown; this is okay. Add more oil if necessary to keep things sizzling. Transfer the fries to a large plate lined with paper towels and cover with another paper towel to keep warm.

4. Add the remaining 1 tbsp olive oil to the pan and quickly arrange the chicken tenders in the pan in a single layer. Follow the same drill as with the potatoes: Don't move the chicken while it browns on the first side, about 3 minutes. Turn the chicken to brown the second side, about 3 minutes longer, adding more oil to the pan if necessary to keep things sizzling.

5. Meanwhile, in a small bowl, combine the remaining 1 tbsp mustard and 1 tbsp mayonnaise and the chutney and stir to mix well. Set the sauce aside.

6. Transfer the chicken fingers as they are cooked to two warmed plates and divide the fries between them. Put the chutney dipping sauce in a small bowl or dollop it on the plates and serve right away.

it's that easy: In order for the fries to cook up tender in the middle and browned on the outside, they must be cut according to the plan. Designate a kitchen ruler and keep it in a handy drawer for measuring. It eliminates guesswork, which equals stress.

extra hungry? A tossed green salad would be a nice accompaniment to this crispy dinner. Just toss whatever greens you have in the crisper drawer with a squirt of lemon, a glug of olive oil, and a sprinkle of salt and pepper and it's done.

in the glass: This feast kind of reminds me of a Happy Meal—even the cornflake coating on the chicken has a trace of sweetness—but for adults. So in the spirit of happiness, how about trying a Gewürztraminer? If you can find it, the Lenz Gewürztraminer from Long Island, New York, is a change of pace from the usual drier whites and embodies the fruit-forward characteristics of this varietal. Try it. It just might make you happy.

Herbed Chicken Paillards

with ZUCCHINI PANCAKES and CHERRY TOMATO PAN SAUCE

The term *paillard* is just shorthand (well, and French) for boneless, skinless chicken breast. Perfectly sautéed and juicy, these chicken breasts are greatly enhanced by the addition of crispy green zucchini pancakes and a freshly sautéed cherry tomato pan sauce enriched with just a touch of butter. Simple, simple, simple. Good, good, good.

1 medium zucchini, grated	*1 large egg*
2 tbsp minced fresh flat-leaf parsley, plus 2 tsp	*2 tbsp unsalted butter, at room temperature*
1 green onion, white and tender green parts, thinly sliced	*1 tbsp minced fresh oregano*
2 garlic cloves, minced	*2 boneless, skinless chicken breast halves, pounded to a 1/2-in/12-mm thickness (see "It's that easy," page 145)*
Salt and freshly ground black pepper	*2 tbsp olive oil*
1/2 cup/55 g panko bread crumbs	*2 cups/340 g cherry tomatoes*

1. In a bowl, combine the zucchini, the 2 tbsp parsley, the green onion, half of the garlic, 1/2 tsp salt, a few grinds of pepper, the panko, and the egg and stir it all together with a fork. The batter should be pretty thick.

2. Combine the remaining garlic, the butter, and oregano in a small bowl and set aside.

3. Pat the chicken dry and sprinkle all over with salt and pepper.

4. Heat a 12-in/30.5-cm skillet over medium-high heat and add the olive oil. When the oil shimmers, add the zucchini batter in 1/4 cup/60 ml mounds. Flatten the pancakes with the back of a fork, pressing them down lightly. Neaten up the sides so that they look nice and cook until the bottoms are crusted and browned, about 3 minutes. Flip with a thin-edged spatula and cook until nicely browned on the second side, about 2 minutes longer. Transfer the pancakes to a platter and cover to keep warm (or place in a low oven).

5. Add half of the herb butter to the hot skillet and lay the chicken pieces in the pan. Cook the chicken, undisturbed, for about 3 minutes, or until you can see pools of liquid forming on the top. Turn the chicken with tongs and cook until it feels firm when you push it with your finger (see "It's that easy"), about 3 minutes longer. Transfer the chicken to the platter with the pancakes and re-cover to keep warm.

6. Add the remaining herb butter and the tomatoes to the pan and cook, stirring occasionally, until the tomatoes burst, about 4 minutes. Smash them partially with a fork and season with salt and pepper.

7. Divide the pancakes between two warmed plates and top with a chicken breast half and the tomato sauce. Sprinkle the 2 tsp parsley over the top and serve hot.

it's that easy: Boneless, skinless chicken breasts have to be the most cooked protein on the planet. The problem is that they are often overcooked. To check for doneness, just press with your fingertips. When cooked, they will feel firm to the touch. Press the tip of your nose. They should feel like that. No more guessing about when they're done.

extra hungry? Baby greens tossed with a splash of balsamic vinegar and a glug of olive oil with blue cheese crumbles scattered over the top would be very tasty with this homey dish.

in the glass: You could drink about any dry white or light-bodied red with this dish. One of my favorite reds is a Pinot Noir from Chalone.

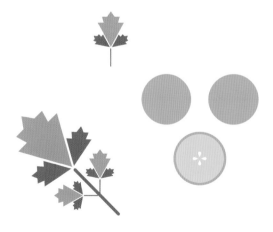

One-Pan Roast Deviled Chicken

with CARROTS, TURNIPS, and PARSNIPS

The "simple is best" maxim resounds in this roasted chicken-and-vegetable dish. One of the reasons it tastes so good may be that many of us rarely eat chicken cooked with the bone in and skin on anymore and have forgotten how tasty chicken can be. A simple mustard coating seals in flavor and contributes tang to the sweet vegetables that lie below, bathing them in the chicken-y goodness.

2 bone-in, skin-on chicken breast halves

Salt and freshly ground black pepper

1 tbsp olive oil, plus more if needed

1 small yellow onion, cut into 8 wedges

2 new potatoes, scrubbed and each cut lengthwise into 8 wedges

2 carrots, cut in half lengthwise and then into 8 pieces about 2 in/5 cm long

2 parsnips, cut in half lengthwise and then into 8 pieces about 2 in/5 cm long

1 turnip, each cut into 8 pieces about 2 in/5 cm long

1 tsp minced fresh rosemary

2 tsp Dijon or whole-grain mustard

1/3 cup/75 ml beer, chicken broth, or water

2 tsp minced fresh flat-leaf parsley

1. Preheat the oven to 400°F/200°C/gas 6. Pat the chicken dry and sprinkle all over with salt and pepper.

2. Heat a 12-in/30.5-cm ovenproof skillet over medium-high heat and add the olive oil. When the oil shimmers, add the chicken, skin-side down, and brown it for about 4 minutes. Don't try to turn the chicken if it's stuck to the bottom of the pan; it will release once it is sufficiently browned. Turn the chicken with tongs and brown the other side for about 3 minutes. Transfer the chicken to a plate. (It won't be fully cooked at this point, but the skin should be nicely browned.)

continued

POULTRY WITH SOUL

141

3. If the pan seems dry, add a little more olive oil. Add the onion, potatoes, carrots, parsnips, turnip, rosemary, 1/2 tsp salt, and a sprinkling of pepper to the hot pan and sauté, stirring every now and then, until the vegetables begin to soften, about 4 minutes. Spread the skin side of the chicken pieces with the mustard and lay them on top of the vegetables, mustard-side up. Transfer to the oven and roast for 10 minutes. Pour the beer into the pan and roast everything until the chicken is cooked through and the vegetables are tender and browned, about 10 minutes longer. Pierce the chicken with a fork to check for tenderness and check the thick part of the breast with an instant-read thermometer. It should read 165°F/74°C.

4. Divide the chicken and vegetables between two warmed plates, sprinkle with the parsley, and serve hot.

it's that easy: It will save you time if you learn to check chicken for doneness by touch. Just get up close and personal with the chicken at different stages of cooking. Press down on it with your finger after it has cooked for 1 minute, 2 minutes, 3 minutes, et cetera, to familiarize yourself with the changes that occur as it cooks. When chicken is done, it should feel firm to the touch—kind of like the tip of your nose. Double-check by inserting an instant-read thermometer into the thickest part (look for a temp of 165°F/74°C) until you get the hang of it.

extra hungry? Add a salad of romaine lettuce, diced apple, dried cranberries, walnuts, a splash of cider vinegar, and a glug of olive oil.

in the glass: The beauty of the wine pairing for this dish is, you can drink just about any wine you're in the mood to quaff. So whatever your favorite, from Bordeaux to Sauvignon Blanc, uncork a bottle and sip away to your heart's content.

Sautéed Chicken Breasts

with LEMON *and* WINTER GREENS

A sautéed chicken breast is one of the fastest and most delicious of meals. It cooks in literally minutes and is perfection with only salt, pepper, and olive oil—but the lemony sauce here is like a little exclamation point of citrusy brightness. As for the greens, I'm especially fond of the rainbow variety of Swiss chard. The stems are yellow, pink, red, or pale green and they look beautiful diced and added to the leaves. You can also use dandelion greens, escarole, frisée, or spinach. (Avoid tougher greens like collard or kale for this dish, since they require longer cooking to reach tenderness.) Perhaps the absolute best, if it's garden season, is a combination of two or three greens—whatever looks good in the produce section.

2 boneless, skinless chicken breast halves, pounded to ½-in/12-mm thickness (see "It's that easy")

Salt and freshly ground black pepper

2 tbsp olive oil

1 shallot, minced

1 bunch chard, leaves cut into thin ribbons, ribs chopped

1 garlic clove, minced

¼ cup/60 ml dry white wine, chicken broth, or water

Zest and juice of ½ lemon

2 tbsp unsalted butter

1 tsp minced fresh flat-leaf parsley

1. Pat the chicken dry and sprinkle all over with salt and pepper.

2. Heat a 12-in/30.5-cm skillet over medium-high heat and add 1 tbsp of the olive oil. When the oil shimmers, add the chicken, "skin-side" down. (Even though there is no skin here, the skin side will be the most attractive side to present on the plate.) Cook, without disturbing, until lightly browned on the first side, about 2 minutes. Don't try to turn the chicken if it's stuck to the bottom of the pan; it will release once it is sufficiently browned. Turn the

continued

chicken and cook it on the second side for another 2 minutes. Transfer the chicken to a plate. (It will not be fully cooked at this point.)

3. Add the remaining 1 tbsp olive oil to the hot pan along with the shallot and chard ribs. Cook until the chard ribs begin to soften, about 1 minute, then sprinkle in 1/4 tsp salt and add a handful of the chard greens. Toss the greens until they wilt. When there is room, add more greens. Continue in this way until all the chard greens are added, tasting and adjusting the seasoning with an occasional sprinkle of salt and pepper as you go. Add the garlic and cook until the greens are completely wilted, about 2 minutes after the last handful is added.

4. Add the wine to the pan and let it come to a simmer. Nestle the partially cooked chicken breasts into the greens. Cover the pan and reduce the heat to low. Simmer the chicken and greens until the chicken is cooked through and the chard is tender, about 3 minutes. Using a slotted spoon, divide the chard between two warmed plates. Place a chicken breast atop each bed of chard. Cover to keep warm (or place in a low oven). There should be some liquid remaining in the pan.

5. Return the skillet to medium-high heat and add the lemon zest and juice. Bring to a boil and cook until the liquid is reduced to about 2 tbsp, about 2 minutes. Add the butter and swirl the pan off heat to melt it. Taste the sauce for seasoning and add a sprinkle of salt and pepper if it needs it.

6. Pour the lemon butter sauce over the chicken and chard, sprinkle the parsley over the top, and serve hot.

it's that easy: To say that today's chicken breasts can be on the large and thick side is an understatement. In order to cook these bigger birds quickly and keep them juicy, you need to pound the breast meat to an even thinness with either a meat pounder or a small, heavy skillet. Just hold the thinner end of the breast with one hand and pound out the thicker end until the whole piece is no more than 1/2 in/12 mm thick. For a tidier process, put the chicken between two sheets of plastic wrap or wax paper. Note: Breast meat that has been frozen and thawed a few times will break down with just a few pounds and might shred a bit, but don't worry. Once cooked, it will look and taste just fine.

extra hungry? Add microwave steam-in-the-bag brown rice. It's especially delicious when the lemony butter sauce mixes with the nutty whole-grain rice.

in the glass: Serve this meal with a glass of chilled South African Sauvignon Blanc from Mulderbosch, or, if you're a die-hard red fan, try an Oregon state Pinot Noir from Wallace Brook.

Pan-Roasted Chicken Leg Quarters

with THYME, SWEET POTATOES, *and* PINEAPPLE

One of the best ways to make whole chicken leg quarters—the thigh-plus-leg pieces—more interesting is to stuff something flavorful between the skin and the meat. This is one of those times when a compound butter (a little butter mashed up with any variety of flavorings) really delivers. In order to keep things simple, I used minced garlic and fresh thyme, but you could try other herb-butter blends and/or add a little grated lemon zest, capers, or shallot the next time you whip up this dish. The sweet potatoes cook up tender and tasty in the chicken's juices and the pineapple adds a touch of sweet and tart that reminds me of those Thanksgiving sweet potato casseroles from our childhood . . . minus the marshmallows, of course.

2 tsp minced fresh flat-leaf parsley

1 tsp minced fresh thyme

1 garlic clove, minced

1 tbsp unsalted butter, at room temperature

2 whole chicken leg quarters (legs and thighs connected, see "It's that easy")

Salt and freshly ground black pepper

1 tbsp olive oil

1 shallot, chopped

2 small or 1 large sweet potato, peeled and cut into 1-in/2.5-cm cubes

1 cup/170 g diced fresh or canned pineapple

1/2 cup/120 ml chicken broth

1. Preheat the oven to 375°F/190°C/gas 5.

2. Combine 1 tsp of the parsley, all of the thyme, the garlic, and butter in a small bowl and mash it all together. Working with one leg quarter at a time,

gently slide your fingers under the skin to separate it from the meat and push half of the herb butter under the skin, pressing it evenly over the surface of the meat. Sprinkle the chicken all over with salt and pepper.

continued

3. Heat a 12-in/30.5-cm ovenproof skillet over medium-high heat and add the olive oil. When the oil shimmers, add the chicken, skin-side down, and brown it on the first side, without moving it, about 3 minutes. Turn and brown the other side, about 3 minutes. Don't try to turn the chicken if it's stuck to the bottom of the pan; it will release once it is sufficiently browned. Transfer to a plate. (It will not be fully cooked at this point.)

4. Carefully pour off all but 2 tbsp of the fat in the pan. (An easy way to accomplish this is to pour the fat over a wad of paper towels in the sink. Once the fat cools, discard the paper towels.) Add the shallot, sweet potatoes, 1/2 tsp salt, and a few grinds of pepper to the oil in the hot pan and sauté until the vegetables begin to soften, about 3 minutes. Add the pineapple and chicken broth and bring to a simmer. Add the chicken and any juices accumulated on the plate, laying the chicken pieces on top of the potatoes. Transfer to the oven and roast the chicken and vegetables until the chicken is cooked through and the potatoes are tender, about 35 minutes.

5. Divide the chicken and potatoes between two warmed plates, sprinkle with the remaining 1 tsp parsley, and serve hot.

it's that easy: If you can't find whole chicken legs, just buy 2 thighs and 2 drumsticks. The meat may cook a little more quickly since the pieces are separated. Check for doneness a few minutes sooner than directed, inserting an instant-read thermometer into the thickest section of the leg. It should read 165°F/74°C for cooked poultry.

extra hungry? Add a serving of microwave steam-in-the-bag green peas. Couldn't be easier.

in the glass: In light of the sweet potatoes and pineapple, a white wine with a touch of sweetness would be my choice here. For fun, search out a bottle of Viognier from Oxford Landing or a Russian River Valley Chardonnay from Michael Pozzan or DeLoach.

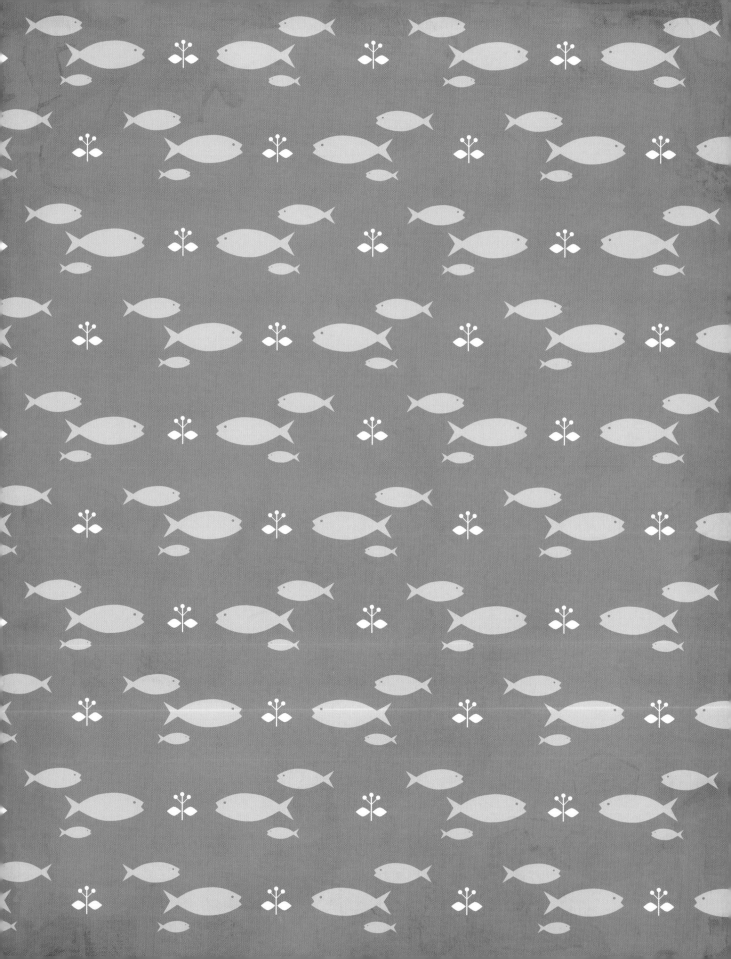

ANGLING FOR MORE

CHAPTER

4

fish dinners

Thyme-Rubbed Salmon

with SHALLOTS and CARAMELIZED CAULIFLOWER "RISOTTO"

Roasted cauliflower is one of the most delectable of vegetables. For years, I made a popular roasted cauliflower gratin in cooking classes; I loved the results so much, I morphed the gratin into a risotto-like dish of delicate, tender, tiny bits of chopped cauliflower. The trick to capturing that roasted flavor is in caramelizing the cauliflower over high heat so that it browns beautifully before being tossed with a little cream. It's positively last-meal-worthy when paired with a simple herb-rubbed salmon. So few ingredients, so much flavor.

Two 6-oz/170-g salmon fillets, skin removed

Salt and freshly ground black pepper

½ tsp minced fresh thyme (see "It's that easy"), plus a few small sprigs for garnish

3 tbsp olive oil

2 shallots, minced

½ head cauliflower, finely chopped

½ cup/120 ml heavy cream

---

1. Pat the fillets dry and sprinkle all over with salt and pepper. Sprinkle the minced thyme over the fish and pat it lightly with your fingers so that it sticks.

2. Heat a 12-in/30.5-cm skillet with a lid over medium-high heat and add 1 tbsp of the olive oil. When the oil shimmers, add the salmon to the pan and cook until browned on the first side, about 2 minutes. Flip the fish with a thin-edged spatula and cook the other side until browned, another minute or so. Transfer the fish to a plate. (It will not be fully cooked at this point.)

3. Add the shallots to the hot pan and sauté until they begin to soften, about 30 seconds. Add the cauliflower, ¼ tsp salt, a few grinds of pepper, and the remaining 2 tbsp olive oil and toss to coat the cauliflower with the oil. Allow the cauliflower to cook undisturbed until it begins to brown, about 3 minutes. Flip the cauliflower over, scraping the bottom of the pan with the spatula, and cook, undisturbed, until the other side browns, another 3 minutes or so. Taste and adjust the seasoning. If the cauliflower is still a little too crunchy for your taste, don't worry. Pour in the cream and give it a stir. It will boil almost immediately. Top the vegetables with the fish. Cover and cook over low heat until the fish flakes easily, about 2 minutes longer.

4. Mound the cauliflower "risotto" into two warmed shallow bowls and top it with the fish. (If you're wondering where the cream went, the cauliflower absorbed most of it up deliciously.) Garnish the plate with the thyme sprigs and serve hot.

it's that easy: *Thyme has woody stems, so it's best to strip the leaves from the stems before chopping them up into a fine mince. To do this, hold the thyme sprig on the tender end and strip the leaves against the grain (that is, in the opposite direction they are pointing) with your other hand. No worries if the tender tip pulls off; those can be minced up with the stripped leaves.*

extra hungry? *How about a salad of red leaf lettuce and halved grape tomatoes with a splash of balsamic and a glug of olive oil?*

in the glass: *A medium-bodied Pinot Noir is a classic pairing with this rich dish. Pinots can be pricey, but there are a few widely available bottles for low prices, such as Definitive or A to Z.*

Citrus-Marinated Salmon

with HEIRLOOM TOMATO CONCASSÉ and GOAT'S-MILK FETA

Concassé is a French term for something that is coarsely chopped, usually tomatoes. It sounds so much more luxurious than "sauce," doesn't it . . . *concassé* . . . Well, this is indeed a luxurious dish of colorful salmon marinated in citrus and dill, with a jammy, tomatoey zucchini sauce and feta cheese topping. It goes without saying that you must make this dish in the summer, when local tomatoes and zucchini are ravishingly fresh and delicious.

1 tbsp minced fresh dill

Zest and juice of ½ large orange

Zest and juice of ½ lemon

Two 6-oz/170-g skin-on salmon fillets

Salt and freshly ground black pepper

2 tbsp olive oil

1 medium red onion, thinly sliced

1 medium zucchini, trimmed, quartered lengthwise, and thinly sliced crosswise

2 large, ripe heirloom tomatoes or other in-season tomatoes, each cored and cut into 8 chunks

1 garlic clove, minced

⅓ cup/75 ml goat's-milk feta cheese (see "It's that easy")

1. Preheat the broiler with the rack in the second position from the top.

2. In a shallow baking dish large enough to hold the salmon fillets, stir together the dill and both citrus zests and juices. Sprinkle the fillets all over with ¼ tsp salt and a few grinds of pepper and add them to the citrus mixture, skin-side up. Set fish aside.

3. Heat a 12-in/30.5-cm ovenproof skillet over medium-high heat and add the olive oil. When the oil shimmers, add the onion and sauté until it softens, about 2 minutes. Add the zucchini and ¼ tsp salt and cook, stirring, until the zucchini begins to soften, about 2 minutes. Add the tomatoes and garlic. The tomatoes will juice up and soften after a minute or so. Continue to cook the vegetables until most of the liquid has evaporated out of the tomatoes and the mixture is thick, about 5 minutes. The goal is to make the *concassé* melt together into a sauce. Taste and season the vegetables with more salt and pepper if it needs it. You may need to reduce the heat if the bottom of the pan threatens to scorch.

4. Spread the vegetables evenly in the pan, top them with the salmon, skin-side down, and pour the citrus mixture over the fish and vegetables. Immediately slip the pan under the broiler and broil until the fish flakes easily with a fork, 7 to 9 minutes, depending on the thickness of the filets. Transfer the fish to two warmed plates, top with the *concassé* and feta, and serve hot.

it's that easy: Feta cheese is usually made with sheep's milk, with a little bit (about 30 percent) of goat's milk blended in. For the record, full-on goat's-milk feta is creamier than the sheep's-milk versions and slightly less tangy. Look for it in the specialty cheese case.

extra hungry? Something green would be refreshing, like an arugula salad with shaved carrot (just use a vegetable peeler), a splash of lemon juice, and a glug of olive oil.

in the glass: Look for a bottle of Louis Jadot Beaujolais-Villages to pair up with this meal. It has the fruit and just enough body to work with the salmon. I like to serve Beaujolais a little more chilled than most reds. Just pop it in the freezer for 10 minutes while you're preparing the meal. It should be just right by the time dinner is on the table.

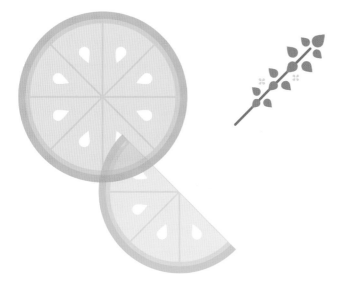

Prosciutto-Wrapped Salmon

with CORN and POBLANO SUCCOTASH

There are few food combos as apt as salmon and corn. Especially when paired with a little air-dried ham, spicy chile, and a touch of cream. You'll love how the prosciutto "shrink-wraps" to the fish and lends its smoky, salty flavor to the creamy corn and chile that lie beneath. This dish is so simple and delicious, you might find yourself doubling the recipe to serve to company next Saturday night. But let them think you slaved in the kitchen for hours. They don't need to know how easy it was to pull this meal together.

Two 6-oz/170-g salmon fillets
(see "It's that easy"), skin removed

Salt and freshly ground black pepper

4 thin slices prosciutto

2 tbsp olive oil

1 small yellow onion, diced

1 poblano chile, seeded, deribbed,
and cut into small dice

Kernels from 2 ears corn or 2 cups/
340 g frozen corn, thawed

1/2 cup/70 g frozen lima beans, thawed

Pinch of cayenne pepper, or more to taste

1/3 cup/75 ml heavy cream
(or chicken broth, if you're watching calories)

1 tbsp thinly sliced fresh basil,
plus a few leaves for garnish

1. Pat the fillets dry and sprinkle lightly with salt and black pepper (not too much salt, because the prosciutto will be salty). Wrap two slices of prosciutto around each fillet, winding it around from top to bottom. Don't worry if it doesn't stick very well; it'll contract and cling to the fish as it cooks. Set the wrapped fish aside.

2. Heat a 12-in/30.5-cm skillet with a lid over medium-high heat and add the olive oil. When the oil shimmers, add the salmon to the pan and cook until browned on the first side, about 2 minutes. Flip the fish over with a thin-edged spatula and cook the other side until browned, another minute or so. Transfer the fish to a plate. (It will not be fully cooked at this point.)

continued

ANGLING FOR MORE

171

vegetables to one side of the pan to make room for the fish.

4. Add the fish to the pan, skin-side down, and cook the fish without moving it for 3 minutes. Flip the fish over with a thin-edged spatula, add the wine, and bring to a simmer. Cover and reduce the heat to low. Simmer the fish and vegetables for 4 minutes. Remove the pan from the heat and let sit for 2 minutes, covered, to allow it to finish cooking gently in the steam and residual heat. You don't want the broccolini to be limp. It should still have some al dente "bite" to it.

5. While the fish and broccolini sit, stir together the yogurt, lemon juice, and mint and season with salt and pepper.

6. Arrange the fish and broccolini on two warmed plates, drizzle with the yogurt sauce, sprinkle with the pistachios, and serve hot.

it's that easy: Garam masala is a blend of Indian spices, and a terrific shortcut to authentic Indian flavor. I've found that one jar of garam masala is a good means for introducing the flavors of India without the expense of buying individual jars of spices like coriander, carda-mom, and turmeric. Look for it in the spice section of your grocery or online.

extra hungry? Add a mound of microwave steam-in-the-bag brown rice.

in the glass: Nothing goes with arctic char like a medium-bodied Pinot Noir. Look for a bottle from the Willamette Valley in Oregon from a producer like Erath. Or if you're feeling flush, the Etude bottling from California will knock your socks off.

Flash-Roasted Tilapia

with NEW POTATOES, PEAS, *and* PESTO MAYONNAISE

One of the reasons I choose tilapia for dinner is that its mild flavor is so versatile. I've kept it simple here, but you know what they say: simple is often best. In this recipe, new potatoes cook up crispy-brown on the outside and fluffy-tender on the inside, while the fish is brushed with a pesto mayonnaise and flash-roasted in a hot oven. The mayo keeps the fish moist and also acts as a dipping sauce for the potatoes. Versatility never tasted so good.

1/4 cup/35 g pine nuts

2 tbsp olive oil

3/4 lb/340 g new potatoes, scrubbed and each cut lengthwise into 6 or 8 wedges

Salt and freshly ground black pepper

2 garlic cloves, roughly chopped

1/2 cup/120 ml mayonnaise

1 tsp fresh lemon juice

1/3 cup/10 g minced fresh basil

1/4 cup/30 g freshly grated Parmesan cheese

Two 6-oz/170-g tilapia fillets

1/2 cup/70 g frozen peas

1. Preheat the oven to 425°F/220°C/gas 7.

2. Put the pine nuts in a dry 12-in/30.5-cm oven-proof skillet over medium heat and toast, tossing the nuts constantly so they don't burn, for about 3 minutes. As soon as they are lightly browned, turn them out onto a plate to cool.

3. Put the skillet over medium-high heat and add the olive oil. When the oil shimmers, add the potatoes and 1/2 tsp salt and season with pepper. Don't

stir the potatoes for the first 3 minutes, then scrape up the browned pieces with a thin-edged spatula and flip them over and brown the other sides, about 2 minutes longer. Sprinkle in the garlic, transfer the pan to the oven, and roast the potatoes until they're almost tender, about 15 minutes.

4. In a bowl, stir together the mayonnaise, lemon juice, basil, and Parmesan. The sauce won't need any salt (because the Parmesan is salty), but add more pepper, if you like.

5. Pat the fillets dry and sprinkle all over with salt and pepper. Spread the pesto mayonnaise over the top of the fish, reserving 2 or 3 tbsp. Remove the potatoes from the oven and sprinkle in the frozen peas. Top the potatoes with the fish, return the pan to the oven, and bake until the fish is cooked and flakes easily with a fork and the potatoes and peas are tender, 10 to 12 minutes.

6. Divide the fish and potatoes between two warmed plates and sprinkle the toasted pine nuts over the top. Put a dollop of extra pesto mayonnaise on each plate for dipping and serve hot.

variation: Tilapia is pretty easy to find, but if there are some beautiful redfish or haddock fillets in the case, go for it. Always choose the freshest, most appealing fish.

it's that easy: Mincing basil is generally a no-no, as all that chopping breaks the tender leaves down to mush. But in this recipe, the basil is minced and added like a pesto to the mayonnaise. I avoid using a food processor on weekdays (because I'd have to wash it), so just combine the hand-chopped basil, lemon, and Parmesan with the mayo and voilà . . . deconstructed pesto mayonnaise.

extra hungry? A salad of leaf lettuce and sun-dried tomatoes with a splash of white wine vinegar, a glug of olive oil, and a few shavings of Parmesan sounds like a nice addition to this meal.

in the glass: Sauvignon Blanc would be my drink of choice here. There are some interesting bottles at great prices from South America. Look for a bottle of Chilean Santa Rita Sauvignon Blanc for a "best buy" value.

....
START TO FINISH
30 minutes
...
HANDS-ON TIME
25 minutes
...
serves 2
....

Miso-Glazed Cod

with WILTED ASIAN RED CABBAGE SLAW

We all have times when we want a simple, light meal with clean, fresh flavors, and this is a meal for those times. Blending up the miso glaze is a snap, and it flavors the flaky cod almost effortlessly with just the right mix of savory and salt. The crunchy slaw is really the star of this show, featuring colorful red cabbage, carrot, tart apple, and peanuts, tossed with rice vinegar, brown sugar, and salt. You asked for it, here it is: light, healthful, and delicious, all in 30 minutes.

2 cups/225 g very thinly sliced red cabbage

1 large carrot, peeled and cut into matchsticks

1 Granny Smith apple, scrubbed, cored, and cut into matchsticks

2 green onions, white and tender green parts, thinly sliced

1/2 cup/15 g chopped fresh cilantro

1 seeded and minced serrano chile, seeds reserved

1/2 cup/70 g peanuts

1 tbsp dry white wine

1 tbsp white miso

2 tsp brown sugar

1 tsp soy sauce

3 tbsp rice vinegar (not seasoned)

Salt

1 tbsp vegetable oil, plus 2 tsp

Two 6-oz/170-g cod fillets

Freshly ground black pepper

1. Preheat the broiler with the rack on the second position from the top.

2. In a large bowl, combine the cabbage, carrot, apple, half of the green onions, the cilantro, serrano, and peanuts and toss to mix well. Set the slaw aside.

3. In a small bowl, combine the wine, miso, 1 tsp of the brown sugar, and the soy sauce and stir well with a fork to make a glaze. Set aside. In another small bowl, stir together the remaining 1 tsp brown sugar, the rice vinegar, 1/2 tsp salt, and 1 tbsp vegetable oil to make a dressing for the slaw. Set the dressing aside.

4. Heat a 12-in/30.5-cm ovenproof skillet over medium-high heat and add the 2 tsp vegetable oil. When the oil shimmers, add the cod fillets to the pan. Cook the fish for 2 minutes without moving them, then carefully spoon the miso glaze over the top of the fish, being careful not to spill any on the bottom of the pan (it will burn). Transfer the pan to the broiler and broil the fish until it is cooked through and the top is golden and glazed, about 5 minutes.

5. Transfer the fish to two warmed plates and return the pan to the heat. Add the slaw dressing and bring to a boil. Quickly pour the hot dressing over the cabbage slaw and toss it for about 1 minute to thoroughly combine the flavors. Taste and add more salt and pepper as desired. For a spicier dish, add the reserved serrano seeds a pinch at a time until you have the heat you want. Mound the slaw alongside the fillets, sprinkle the remaining green onion over the top, and serve hot.

it's that easy: Dense cabbage and carrot usually need some time in the vinegary dressing to tenderize, but heating up the dressing helps it to penetrate the crunchy vegetables and flavor them more quickly. If the slaw doesn't wilt a little when tossed with the hot dressing, just remember to cut everything a little thinner the next time.

extra hungry? Add microwave steam-in-the-bag rice, either brown or white, on those hungrier-than-usual nights.

in the glass: Look for a lean, crisp Pinot Gris from Oregon. You might be more familiar with its Italian cousin, Pinot Grigio, but a bottle from Oregon's King Estate or Eyrie Vinyards will satisfy with apple, pear, and melon flavors—perfect with the slaw.

START TO FINISH
25 minutes
...
HANDS-ON TIME
20 minutes
...
serves 2

Black Cod Fillets

poached in FIVE-SPICE BROTH with BABY BOK CHOY and UDON

I could eat a meal like this almost every night. It's light and fresh, with vegetables and flaky fish poached in a perfumed broth. Five-spice powder is a Chinese spice blend combining equal parts cinnamon, star anise, clove, fennel, and Szechuan peppercorns, and can be found these days in most well-stocked grocery stores. A spa meal without the sacrifice, the chewy udon noodles and bok choy soak up that brothy flavor and round out this quick meal perfectly. Who said eating well was hard work?

Two 6-oz/170-g black cod fillets

Salt and freshly ground black pepper

1 3/4 cups/420 ml chicken broth

1 tbsp dry sherry

1 tsp soy sauce, plus more if needed

1 tsp sugar

1 tsp five-spice powder

1 tsp toasted sesame oil

1 tbsp vegetable oil

3 heads baby bok choy, cored and thinly sliced on the diagonal (see "It's that easy"), leaves separated from stalks

1 carrot, peeled and thinly sliced on the diagonal (see "It's that easy")

1 tbsp peeled and minced fresh ginger

3 oz/85 g udon noodles

1 green onion, white and tender green parts, thinly sliced on the diagonal (see "It's that easy")

2 tsp minced fresh cilantro

1 tsp sesame seeds

1. Pat the fillets dry and sprinkle all over with salt and pepper.

2. In a small bowl, whisk together the chicken broth, sherry, soy sauce, sugar, five-spice powder, and sesame oil. Set aside.

3. Heat a 12-in/30.5-cm skillet with a lid over medium-high heat and add the vegetable oil. When the oil shimmers, add the bok choy stems, carrot, and ginger and sauté until the bok choy turns bright green and the ginger is fragrant, about 2 minutes.

continued

Add the broth mixture and bring to a simmer. Add the noodles and give them a stir to keep them from sticking. When the broth returns to a simmer, top the noodles and veggies with the fish, bok choy leaves, and green onion. Cover, reduce the heat to low, and simmer until the noodles and fish are tender and cooked through, about 4 minutes. Taste and add more soy sauce or pepper if the mix needs it.

4. Divide the noodles and fish between two warmed shallow bowls and ladle the broth and vegetables over. Garnish with the cilantro and sesame seeds and serve hot.

variation: If you can't find black cod, don't despair. This dish is delicious using cod or tilapia as well.

it's that easy: Cutting vegetables on the diagonal is an Asian technique that exposes more cut surface to heat, helping the vegetables to cook faster. They also look prettier cut that way. Just angle your knife and slice away. You'll get the hang of it in no time.

extra hungry? Serve a bigger piece of fish. About 8 oz/225 g should do it.

in the glass: Try a Sauvignon Blanc from New Zealand, such as Kim Crawford or Pomelo for tropical fruit and a zesty finish.

Baked Halibut

with WARN FENNEL-ZUCCHINI CHOPPED SALAD

Because of its firm, meaty texture, I think of halibut as the strip steak of fish. Its light fresh taste is perfectly delicious in this, one of my favorite incarnations—cooked over a bed of browned potatoes with a shower of herbed, lemony vegetables steaming on top. The "salad" of lemon, capers, fennel, and zucchini releases flavorful juices and perfumes the fish and potatoes as they steam in a hot, hot oven.

Two 6-oz/170-g halibut fillets, (see "It's that easy")

Salt and freshly ground black pepper

1 small fennel bulb, trimmed, cored, and thinly sliced

1 small zucchini, trimmed, halved lengthwise, and thinly sliced crosswise

8 Kalamata olives, pitted and halved

1 tsp capers, rinsed, patted dry, and roughly chopped

1 garlic clove, minced

1 tsp minced fresh thyme leaves

2 tsp fresh lemon juice, plus zest of ½ lemon, plus more for garnish (optional)

2 tbsp extra-virgin olive oil

3 new potatoes, scrubbed, halved, and very thinly sliced

1. Preheat the oven to 450°F/230°C/gas 8. Pat the fillets dry and sprinkle all over with salt and pepper.

2. In a medium bowl, combine the fennel, zucchini, olives, capers, garlic, thyme, lemon juice and zest, 1 tbsp of the olive oil, 1/4 tsp salt, and a few grinds of pepper. Toss the vegetables to combine the flavors. Set aside.

3. Heat a 12-in/30.5-cm ovenproof skillet with a lid over medium-high heat and add the remaining 1 tbsp olive oil. When the oil shimmers, add the potatoes to the pan and spread in a single layer. Sprinkle them with salt and pepper and cook until crispy on the bottom, about 4 minutes. Turn the potatoes with a thin-edged spatula and top them with the halibut fillets. Pour the marinated

continued

vegetable mixture over the top and spread it in an even layer (the liquid accumulated in the bowl will make the pan spatter). Cover and cook for about 3 minutes, then transfer the pan to the oven. Bake until the fish flakes easily with a fork, about 15 minutes.

4. Divide the fish and vegetables between two warmed plates. Sprinkle with the extra lemon zest, if desired, and serve hot.

variation: Utilize other vegetables you may have on hand—maybe some thinly sliced carrots or cauliflower, or chopped grape tomatoes or broccoli. Remember that the fish cooks very quickly, so cut the vegetables into thin or small pieces to ensure that they'll be tender when the fish is done. Other fish to substitute are salmon, cod, tilapia, or trout. And please freely swap out other herbs such as basil, rosemary, or tarragon.

it's that easy: When choosing fish for dinner, I like to check the Monterey Bay Aquarium Seafood Watch, www.montereybayaquarium.org for help in making healthful choices for dinner and for our oceans. It contains information about what fish to avoid (because of overfishing, PCBs, how they are caught) and healthful alternatives to that particular fish. Check it out. You'll learn lots.

extra hungry? The best loaf of bread you can find, a plate of extra-virgin olive oil, French gray sea salt, and a few grinds of pepper would make this meal even more heavenly.

in the glass: I've had a white Côtes du Rhône with this meal and enjoyed it very much. Look for an affordable white like the Parallèle 45 Côtes du Rhône Villages from Jaboulet for balance and fresh acidity.

Poached Halibut

with CHIVE GREMOLATA, BRUSSELS SPROUTS, *and* BUTTER BEAN MASH

If you're looking for a healthful, low-fat dinner that just about cooks all by itself, look no further. The meal starts off with poached halibut and a lemon, garlic, and chive gremolata topping that sets it off simply and flavorfully. I love butter beans and never get over the ease of opening up a can of these creamy beauties to act as a starchy base for the fish, Brussels sprouts, and broth. It *is* possible to eat food that's healthful, easy to cook, and delicious at the same time. Who knew?

Zest of 1 lemon

½ tsp minced garlic

1 tbsp minced fresh chives (see "It's that easy")

1 cup/200 g canned butter beans, drained and rinsed (see Tip, page 131)

Two 6-oz/170-g halibut fillets

Salt and freshly ground black pepper

1 tbsp olive oil

1 shallot, sliced

15 Brussels sprouts, quartered and cored

1 ½ cups/360 ml chicken or vegetable broth

1. In a small bowl, stir together the lemon zest, garlic, and chives. Set the gremolata aside.

2. Divide the beans between two microwave-safe shallow soup bowls (or other individual serving bowls) and set them aside.

3. Pat the fillets dry and sprinkle all over with salt, pepper, and half the gremolata. Set aside.

4. Heat a 12-in/30.5-cm skillet with a lid over medium-high heat and add the olive oil. When the oil shimmers, add the shallot and cook it until it softens, about 1 minute. Add the Brussels sprouts, ¼ tsp salt, and a few grinds of pepper and sauté until the sprouts turn bright green, about 2 minutes. Add the broth and bring to a simmer. Slide the fillets into the simmering broth. Cover the pan and poach until the fish is cooked through and the sprouts are tender, about 10 minutes. When done, the fish will flake easily when pulled apart with the tines of a fork.

5. When the fish is almost done poaching, sprinkle a few pinches of the remaining gremolata over each reserved bowl of beans and microwave them for about 1 minute to heat the beans up. Mash the warm beans lightly with the back of a fork.

6. When the fish is done, carefully scoop it from the broth with a wide spatula and transfer it to the bowls. Scoop out the sprouts and divide them between the bowls, then ladle in the broth. Garnish with the remaining gremolata and serve hot.

it's that easy: Gremolata is usually made of parsley, lemon zest, and garlic. I just happen to have lots of chives growing in my herb patch, so I used them here for the green in place of parsley. If you have parsley on hand or prefer it, go ahead and use it. Other fresh herbs that could be swapped in are basil, marjoram, or oregano.

extra hungry? Ciabatta bread drizzled with olive oil and toasted in your toaster is an easy fix for extra-hungry nights.

in the glass: A smooth and creamy white with nice acid would be delicious with this lemony, garlicky fish. Look for an inexpensive but delicious bottle of Chardonnay from Edna Valley, such as Hess or Mirassou.

Haddock

with SHIITAKE MUSHROOMS and BLACK-EYED PEA RAGÙ

I became very fond of haddock after spending some time in Maine. Of course the catch was gloriously fresh up there, and that might be the secret to becoming enamored of certain fish: that you've eaten them just moments away from swimming in the ocean. Here, I've jazzed my fave fish with some Cajun seasoning and paired it with a Southern ragù of simmered black-eyed peas, bacon, and shiitake mushrooms for a little Maine by way of Louisiana. Thanks to Stephen Stryjewski of Cochon for the inspiration of this recipe.

Two 6-oz/170-g haddock fillets

Salt and freshly ground black pepper

1/2 tsp Cajun seasoning (see "It's that easy")

1 tbsp olive oil

2 slices bacon

1 small yellow onion, thinly sliced

1 carrot, peeled and thinly sliced

1 celery stalk, quartered lengthwise and thinly sliced crosswise

4 oz/115 g shiitake mushrooms (see "It's that easy"), brushed clean and thinly sliced

1 garlic clove, minced

1/2 tsp dried thyme

Pinch of red pepper flakes

One 15 1/2-oz/445-g can black-eyed peas, drained and rinsed

3/4 cup/180 ml low-sodium chicken broth

1 tbsp unsalted butter

2 tsp minced fresh chives

1. Pat the fillets dry and sprinkle a little salt and black pepper on both sides. Sprinkle the Cajun seasoning over the tops.

2. Heat a 12-in/30.5-cm skillet with a lid over medium-high heat and add the olive oil. When the oil shimmers, add the bacon and cook, turning as needed, until crispy, 5 to 7 minutes total. Transfer to paper towels to drain, and crumble it once it's cooled.

3. Add the fish to the hot fat in the pan and cook until the fillets are browned on the bottom, 2 to 3 minutes. Carefully flip with a thin-edged spatula and brown the second side, about 2 minutes longer. Transfer the fish to a plate and cover to keep warm. (It will not be cooked through at this point.)

4. Add the onion, carrot, celery, mushrooms, garlic, thyme, ¼ tsp salt, and red pepper flakes to the hot pan and sauté until the vegetables begin to soften, about 3 minutes. Add the black-eyed peas and chicken broth and bring to a simmer. Cover and reduce the heat to low. Simmer until the vegetables are almost tender, about 3 minutes. Taste the ragù and add more salt, black pepper, or red pepper flakes if it needs it. Return the fish to the pan, Cajun-spiced-side up, and dot it with the butter. Cover and simmer until the fish is cooked through, another 5 minutes or so.

5. Scoop the black-eyed pea ragù onto two warmed plates and top it with the fish. Sprinkle the chives and bacon over the top and serve right away.

variation: If you can't find haddock, use hake or cod.

it's that easy: Cajun seasoning is a punchy blend of paprika, salt, celery, sugar, garlic, black pepper, red pepper, onion, oregano, caraway, dill, turmeric, cumin, bay, mace, cardamom, basil, marjoram, rosemary, and thyme. You can sprinkle it on just about anything.

Shiitake mushrooms have a tough stem that must be removed before slicing and cooking. Unlike many mushroom stems, these will never tenderize, so pull them off and throw them away.

extra hungry? A light salad of Bibb lettuce and arugula with a squirt of lemon, a glug of olive oil, and a scattering of clementine or orange segments sounds just right.

in the glass: A buttery Chardonnay from Geyser Peak would be a light and refreshing accompaniment to this hearty meal.

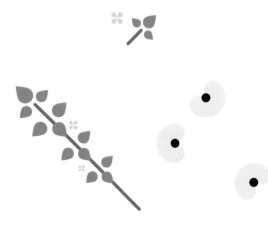

Catfish Tacos

with CHIPOTLE SLAW

My siblings and I used to fish for catfish in the Ohio River when we were kids. As soon as we caught them, we'd throw them back into the murky waters, waiting for the next "big one" to take the line. Today catfish are farm-raised, and these delicious fish are perfect for fish tacos because they're firm and hold their shape. The crunch and smoky spice of the red-and-white chipotle slaw is my favorite filling to go with these crispy fillets all wrapped up in a warm tortilla. No need to drop a line.

1 tsp minced chipotle pepper in adobo sauce (see "It's that easy")

1/4 cup/60 ml mayonnaise

1 tbsp honey

2 tsp fresh lime juice

Salt and freshly ground black pepper

1 cup/115 g very thinly sliced white cabbage

1 cup/115 g very thinly sliced red cabbage

1 green onion, white and tender green parts, thinly sliced

1 large egg

2 tsp hot sauce

1 cup/110 g panko bread crumbs, plus more if needed

1/4 cup/30 g all-purpose flour

8 to 10 oz/225 to 280 g catfish fillets

1/2 cup/120 ml vegetable oil

Four or five 10-in/25-cm flour tortillas

1. In a large bowl, combine the chipotle, mayonnaise, honey, lime juice, 1/4 tsp salt, and a few grinds of pepper and stir well to mix. Add both cabbages and the green onion and toss and stir to combine and coat the vegetables well with the chipotle mayonnaise. Set aside.

2. In a large, shallow bowl, whisk together the egg with a splash of water, a pinch of salt, and the hot sauce. Pour the panko and flour onto two separate large plates. Pat the fillets dry and sprinkle all over with salt and pepper.

continued

3. Dredge the fish in the flour and knock off the excess. Dip the fish into the egg to coat it completely and then coat it thoroughly with the panko. Place the fillets on a platter as they are breaded.

4. Heat a 12-in/30.5-cm skillet over medium-high heat and add the vegetable oil. When the oil shimmers and is very hot, slip the breaded fish into the pan and brown it on one side, about 3 minutes. Turn and brown the other side, another 3 minutes. Transfer the fish to paper towels to drain.

5. Pour off the oil in the pan (pouring it into a metal can in the sink works well) and return the pan to the heat. Dump the slaw mixture into the pan and toss it for about 1 minute to warm it up. Don't cook it so long that it completely wilts. You want it to have a little crunch. Return the slaw to the bowl so that it doesn't overcook.

6. Warm the tortillas wrapped in microwavable plastic wrap until soft and pliable, 20 to 30 seconds. Lay the fish down the center of the tortillas and top it with the slaw. Wrap in the sides and bottom and eat these fish tacos with your hands. Use lots of napkins.

variation: Other fish to fry are cod, tilapia, or even salmon cut into wide strips.

it's that easy: Chipotles are smoked jalapeño chiles, usually packed in adobo, a spicy tomato sauce. You can rarely use the whole can in a recipe because they are quite hot, so I freeze the remaining chiles in zippered plastic freezer bags to use another time. You can find canned chipotles in Latin groceries and well-stocked supermarkets. Be cautious when handling the chiles, as they can be quite hot. Wear gloves if you are sensitive or try not to touch them with your fingers too much.

extra hungry? Since you're eating this meal with your hands, how about pairing it with a bowl of your favorite potato chips?

in the glass: A Spanish Albariño would be my choice here. It has the acidity to cut the richness of the tacos but with a softer, creamy edge.

Panko-Fried Crab Cakes

with HEIRLOOM TOMATO, NECTARINE, *and* AVOCADO SALAD

Even if your store-bought tomatoes aren't as good as Grandpa used to grow, the nectarine's bright acid is guaranteed to liven up this salad dressed in a simple pesto vinaigrette. The cooking part of this recipe is a fairly traditional crab cake, with just enough bread crumbs and mayo to lightly hold it together. The avocado is the unifying force that makes this salad such a charmer. Grandpa would be so proud.

2 tbsp minced green onion

2 tbsp minced red bell pepper

2 tbsp minced celery

2 tbsp mayonnaise

1 tbsp fresh lemon juice, plus 1 tsp lemon zest

1 tsp Dijon mustard

Salt and freshly ground black pepper

8 oz/225 g fresh backfin or lump crabmeat, picked over for shell fragments (see "It's that easy")

1 egg white, beaten

1/3 cup/40 g panko bread crumbs, plus 1/2 cup/55 g

1 tbsp pesto, purchased or homemade

1 tbsp balsamic vinegar

4 tbsp/60 ml olive oil

2 handfuls baby greens (I buy them already washed)

1 heirloom tomato (or the best you can find), sliced

1 nectarine, pitted and sliced

1/2 ripe avocado, peeled and sliced (see "It's that easy," page 60)

1. In a large bowl, combine the green onion, bell pepper, celery, mayonnaise, lemon juice and zest, mustard, 1/2 tsp salt, and a grind or two of pepper and stir to mix well. Add the crabmeat, egg white, and 1/3 cup/40 g panko. Toss lightly to combine the crab with the veggies and flavorings, but not so much that you break down all the nice chunks of crab. Form the crab mixture into four cakes about 3/4 in/2 cm thick. If the mixture is too loose to form into cakes, refrigerate it for about 15 minutes so it

continued

firms up. Pour the ½ cup/55 g panko onto a plate and press the cakes into the crumbs on both sides so that they adhere. Refrigerate the cakes on a plate while you assemble the salad.

2. Combine the pesto, vinegar, a sprinkle of salt, a grind or two of pepper, and 2 tbsp olive oil in a small bowl and whisk to blend well. Set it aside.

3. Arrange the greens on two chilled plates and top them with the tomato, nectarine, and avocado. Drizzle the pesto vinaigrette over the salads and set them aside while you fry the crab cakes.

4. Heat a 12-in/30.5-cm skillet over medium-high heat and add the remaining 2 tbsp olive oil. When the oil shimmers, carefully slide the crab cakes into the pan and fry for 3 minutes on the first side, flip them over with a thin-edged spatula and cook on the second side until they are browned on the outside and hot and creamy on the inside, another 2 or 3 minutes. If the cakes are browning too fast, turn off the heat and let them sit in the pan for a few minutes so they continue to heat through. Transfer the crab cakes to the top of the greens and serve the salads immediately. The greens will wilt a little from the heat of the crab cake, but it will be a good thing. I promise.

it's that easy: Thank heavens there's no need to crack open a crab and manually pick out the meat. Phillips, a widely available purveyor of high-quality, fresh-packed crabmeat, has done all the messy work for you. Look for Phillips or other good brands in 8-oz/225-g plastic containers in the refrigerated case at your fishmonger or supermarket.

extra hungry? How about a few slices of focaccia from your local bakery? Anything cheesy would be delicious with all the fresh flavors in the salad.

in the glass: The tart tastes in this salad look for a corresponding tartness in the accompanying wine. Frog's Leap Sauvignon Blanc is widely distributed and a fine wine for the price.

Stir-Fried Ginger Shrimp

with SUGAR SNAP PEAS, RED BELL PEPPERS, *and* CORN

Shrimp, also known by the catchall "prawns" in the United Kingdom and other places, are a great foundation for a feed-me-fast meal, because they cook so quickly. But did you know that shrimp also absorbs the flavor of marinades in a snap as well? Just a short marinating time in fresh ginger, garlic, soy sauce, and chili garlic sauce infuses the shrimp in this stir-fry with a big blast of flavor. They're a great combo with the crispy, bright green sugar snap peas, sweet red pepper, fresh cut corn, and a hint of sesame. Cooking fast never tasted so good. Just be sure to *eat* it slow.

2 tbsp peeled and minced fresh ginger

2 garlic cloves, minced

2 tbsp soy sauce

1 1/2 tsp chili garlic sauce, plus more to taste

About 16 uncooked large shrimp, peeled and deveined

2/3 cup/165 ml chicken broth

1 tsp toasted sesame oil

1 tsp honey

2 tbsp vegetable oil

8 oz/225 g sugar snap peas, strings removed (see "It's that easy")

2 green onions, white and green parts, thinly sliced

1 small red bell pepper, seeded, deribbed, and cut into 1/2-in/12-mm dice

Kernels from 1 ear corn or 1 cup/170 g frozen corn, thawed

1/4 cup/10 g minced fresh cilantro

Microwave steam-in-the-bag rice for serving

1 tsp sesame seeds

1. In a bowl, combine half of the ginger, half of the garlic, 1 tsp of the soy sauce, and 1 tsp of the chili garlic sauce and stir to mix well. Add the shrimp and toss to coat with the spice paste. Set aside.

2. Whisk together 1 tbsp soy sauce and 1/2 tsp chili garlic sauce, the chicken broth, sesame oil, and honey in a small bowl. Set aside.

3. Heat a 12-in/30.5-cm skillet over medium-high heat and add the vegetable oil. When the oil shimmers, add the remaining ginger and garlic, the snap peas, green onions, and bell pepper and sauté, stirring, until the veggies are almost cooked through, about 4 minutes. Add the shrimp with their marinade, the broth mixture, and corn and cook for another 3 minutes, stirring to cook the shrimp. Stir in the cilantro. Taste for seasoning and add the remaining soy sauce if it needs it. If you'd like more heat, stir in more chili garlic sauce in very small increments, tasting as you go.

4. Mound the cooked rice on two warmed plates and top it with the stir-fry and a sprinkle of sesame seeds. Serve hot.

it's that easy: Stir-fries are among the speediest of meals to prepare. They're a great excuse to use up your best local farmers' market finds because there are so many different veggies you can swap in. Be inventive. That's how the best dishes happen. To de-string the peas, just pinch the ends and pull. The strings will come right off.

extra hungry? How about a cup of ramen on the side?

in the glass: A Chardonnay would work here. Look for food-friendly bottlings from Joel Gott for value, fruit, and a little less oak than usual.

Scallops

and ASIAN NOODLE SALAD *with* SPICY LIME SAUCE

The more I work with rice-stick noodles, the more I love them. They're just so darn versatile. But, really, in this recipe the noodles are merely a vehicle for the limy sauce, crunchy vegetables, and chopped herbs. Did I mention the peanuts? Oh, and how about the scallops . . . cooked to a perfect crispy brown on the outside, but tender and silky on the inside. Oh, yeah, there's a lot more going on here than just noodles.

4 oz/115 g rice-stick noodles

4 oz/115 g snow peas, thinly sliced on the diagonal

½ cucumber, peeled, seeded, and sliced into matchsticks

1 green onion, thinly sliced

¼ cup/28 g shredded carrot

¼ cup/32 g chopped peanuts

2 tbsp chopped cilantro

2 tbsp chopped basil

2 tbsp chopped mint

3 tbsp water

2 tbsp fish sauce

2 tbsp sugar

3 tbsp lime juice, plus more if necessary, plus ½ lime, quartered

½ tsp red chili flakes, plus more if necessary

½ tsp chili garlic sauce

1 garlic clove, minced

Salt

14 oz/400 g day-boat scallops (also called dry or dry-packed), patted dry on paper towels

Salt and freshly ground black pepper

2 tbsp vegetable oil

1. In a heatproof bowl, soak the noodles in boiling water until they are softened, about 15 minutes. Drain the noodles.

2. Combine the noodles with the snow peas, cucumber, green onion, carrot, peanuts, cilantro, basil, and mint in a medium bowl.

3. Combine the water, fish sauce, sugar, lime juice, red chili flakes, chili garlic sauce, and garlic in a small bowl and stir to dissolve the sugar.

4. Reserve 1 tbsp of the sauce and add the rest to the noodles, tossing to blend. Taste and adjust the seasoning with salt, chili flakes, or lime juice.

5. Sprinkle the scallops with salt and pepper on both sides.

6. Heat a 12-in/30.5-cm skillet over medium-high heat and add the vegetable oil. When the oil shimmers, add the scallops. Cook until browned on the first side, about 2 minutes (don't try to move them sooner or they will stick and tear). Using tongs or a spatula, carefully turn them over and sear the second side for another 2 minutes. They should be browned and slightly firm to the touch when pressed with a finger. Remove the pan from the heat.

7. Arrange the noodle salad on individual plates and top with the browned scallops. Drizzle the reserved sauce over the scallops and garnish with the lime quarters. Serve right away.

it's that easy: One of my favorite kitchen gadgets is a ¼-cup/60-ml spouted measuring cup with incremental markings. It comes in really handy when measuring out the ingredients for an Asian sauce by the tablespoon. No more awkward measuring spoons. Look for them in cookware shops or online and buy a few. You'll use them every day.

extra hungry? Add ½ cup/85 g halved grape tomatoes or thinly sliced bell pepper to the noodle salad.

in the glass: There's a lot going on in the flavor department here. I'd go with a German Spatlese–style Reisling since its medium body and acidity go well with most Asian-inspired dishes. The labels on German wines are notoriously confusing so do yourself a favor and just ask the wine guy for a not too dry, not too sweet, refreshing, food-friendly bottle. Try a different label each time. Be an explorer. You'll be sure to discover something great.

Salade Niçoise

Salade niçoise, as its many passionate fans know, is much more than a salad. It's one of those dishes that's been filling up hungry laborers for centuries—the potatoes, green beans, tomatoes, and wedges of hard-boiled egg absorb the herb-infused vinaigrette, while the roasted peppers, anchovies, and tuna create a kind of chunky sauce. For the physically or mentally exhausted, it's just the thing to fill you up after a hard day, and for lovers of salad as a meal, it's the perfect dish for a picnicky summer Sunday.

1 ½ tbsp white wine vinegar

½ tsp Dijon mustard

1 tbsp minced mixed fresh herbs, such as thyme, basil, parsley, and chives

Salt and freshly ground black pepper

¼ cup/60 ml extra-virgin olive oil

4 red-skinned new potatoes, scrubbed and each cut into 6 wedges

4 oz/115 g green beans, trimmed and snapped in two

3 handfuls mixed salad greens (I buy them already washed)

One 5-oz/140-g can olive oil–packed tuna, preferably imported, drained

1 ½ cups/255 g halved grape or cherry tomatoes

¼ cup/55 g jarred roasted red peppers, drained and cut into strips

¼ cup/40 g Niçoise or Kalamata olives

1 hard-boiled egg (I use store-bought to save time), peeled and quartered

8 anchovy fillets (see "It's that easy"), rinsed and patted dry if salt-packed

1. Fill a 12-in/30.5-cm skillet with water up to about 1 in/2.5 cm from the top and bring to a boil over medium-high heat.

2. Meanwhile, in a medium bowl, whisk together the vinegar, mustard, herbs, ¼ tsp salt, a few grinds

of pepper, and the olive oil. Taste and add more salt and pepper if it needs it. Set the dressing aside.

3. When the water boils, add ½ tsp salt and the potatoes. Return to a boil and cook the potatoes for 3 minutes. Reduce the heat to medium, add the green beans, and cook until the beans are crisp-tender and the potatoes are easily pierced with the tip of a knife, another 5 minutes or so. Drain the potatoes and beans in a colander set in the sink and run cold water over them to cool them down slightly.

4. Add the cooked potatoes and beans to the bowl with the dressing and toss gently to coat. Taste and adjust the seasoning.

5. Arrange the greens on two plates or one big platter and top them with the dressed potatoes and green beans, reserving the dressing. Scatter the tuna, tomatoes, roasted peppers, olives, egg quarters, and anchovies attractively over the greens. Sprinkle salt and a few grinds of pepper over all. Drizzle the remaining dressing liberally over the salad and serve right away.

it's that easy: Ahhh, anchovies. Cartoon cats aren't the only ones who dream of them. But love them or leave them, they do add a certain something-something to dishes. If you are in the leave-them camp, please try the salt-packed variety at least once. They're firmer and less, ahem, fragrant. Just rinse off the salt and toss them in the salad. You might be surprised at the flavor they add.

extra hungry? Extra-easy: Just add bread and extra-virgin olive oil sprinkled with gray sea salt for dipping.

in the glass: In the spirit of alfresco dining in the south of France, what could be better than a rosé. Of course a bottle of Bandol would be ideal, but you won't go wrong with Domaine du Roquefort Rose de Provence Corail. It has lots of strawberry and orange but a dry finish that works especially well with the blast of flavor in this dish.

find it fast

dinner in 30 minutes or less

- Balsamic Turkey with Artichokes and Eggplant Caponata, 128
- Barley and Lentil Salad with Dried Cranberries and Walnuts, 40
- Black Cod Fillets Poached in Five-Spice Broth with Baby Bok Choy and Udon, 181
- Catfish Tacos with Chipotle Slaw, 191
- Citrus-Marinated Salmon with Heirloom Tomato Concassé and Goat's-Milk Feta, 168
- Croque Madame, 54
- Cuban Sandwiches, 56
- Flat-Iron Steak with Green Beans, Chili-Hoisin Sauce, and Sesame Seeds, 94
- Fluffy Spring Frittata with Asparagus, Bell Peppers, and Gruyère, 118
- Fresh Pepper Linguine with Olive Oil–Packed Tuna, Capers, and Golden Raisins, 28
- Linguine with Chicken, Spinach, and Feta Cheese, 26
- Lo Mein Noodles with Chicken, Snow Peas, and Peanut Sauce, 34
- Miso-Glazed Cod with Wilted Asian Red Cabbage Slaw, 178
- Pan-Fried Arctic Char with Garam Masala, Broccolini, and Yogurt Sauce, 173
- Pasta Carbonara, 30
- Poached Halibut with Chive Gremolata, Brussels Sprouts, and Butter Bean Mash, 186
- Prosciutto-Wrapped Salmon with Corn and Poblano Succotash, 171
- Scallops and Asian Noodle Salad with Spicy Lime Sauce, 198
- Spinach-and-Cheese Tortellini with Leeks and Creamy Mushroom Sauce, 32
- Sweet-and-Sour Stir-Fry with Beef, Broccoli, and Mango, 88
- Thai Red Curry Chicken with Bell Peppers and Broccoli, 150
- Thyme-Rubbed Salmon with Shallots and Caramelized Cauliflower "Risotto," 166

- Turkey Chili with Poblano and Queso Fresco, 130
- Turkey Tonkatsu with Cabbage, Portobellos, and Pickled Ginger, 126
- Veal Piccata with Brussels Sprout Hash and Apples, 104
- Veal Saltimbocca with Asparagus, Lemon, and Israeli Couscous, 106
- Wild Mushroom Frittata with Cheddar, Green Onions, and Peas, 123
- Winter Frittata with Escarole, Bacon, and Feta Cheese, 121

spring forward (spring meals)

- Baked Halibut with Warm Fennel-Zucchini Chopped Salad, 183
- Braised Chicken Thighs with Wild Rice, Walnuts, and Grapes, 152
- Catfish Tacos with Chipotle Slaw, 191
- Cornflake-Crusted Chicken Fingers with Rosemary–Sweet Potato Pan Fries and Chutney Dipping Sauce, 135
- Croque Madame, 54
- Cuban Sandwiches, 56
- Fettuccine with Scallops, Carrots, and Ginger-Lime Butter Sauce, 24
- Flank Steak with Chimichurri and Summer Squash Hash, 97
- Fluffy Spring Frittata with Asparagus, Bell Peppers, and Gruyère, 118
- Fresh Pepper Linguine with Olive Oil–Packed Tuna, Capers, and Golden Raisins, 28
- Golden Corn Cakes with Crispy Pancetta and Arugula Salad, 70
- Lemony Risotto with Asparagus, Carrots, and Chives, 45
- Lo Mein Noodles with Chicken, Snow Peas, and Peanut Sauce, 34
- Miso-Glazed Cod with Wilted Asian Red Cabbage Slaw, 178
- Mujaddara with Onions, Dried Apricots, Almonds, and Spicy Yogurt, 52
- Pad Thai, 36
- Pan-Fried Arctic Char with Garam Masala, Broccolini, and Yogurt Sauce, 173
- Quick Choucroute Garni, 66
- Rosemary Chicken Leg Quarters with Orange Gremolata, 158

- Salade Niçoise, 200
- Sautéed Pork Chops with Sweet Potato, Apple, and Mustard Sauce, 79
- Scallops and Asian Noodle Salad with Spicy Lime Sauce, 198
- Skirt Steak Fajitas with Pico de Gallo and Avocado, 90
- Spicy Pork Stir-Fry with Lime, Cashews, and Noodles, 84
- Tuna Burgers with Wasabi Mayo and Quick Cucumber Pickle, 61
- Turkey Tonkatsu with Cabbage, Portobellos, and Pickled Ginger, 126
- Veal Saltimboca with Asparagus, Lemon, and Israeli Couscous, 106
- Vegetable Biryani with Green Beans, Cauliflower, and Carrots, 50
- Yellow Curry Chicken with Green Beans and Potatoes, 148

hot town summer in the city (summer meals)

- Balsamic Turkey with Artichokes and Eggplant Caponata, 128
- Catfish Tacos with Chipotle Slaw, 191
- Citrus-Marinated Salmon with Heirloom Tomato Concassé and Goat's-Milk Feta, 168
- Fettuccine with Scallops, Carrots, and Ginger-Lime Butter Sauce, 24
- Flank Steak with Chimichurri and Summer Squash Hash, 97
- Fresh Summer Pasta with Tomatoes, Garlic, Basil, and Buttery Croutons, 21
- Fried Green Tomato Sandwiches with Bacon and Chutney, 59
- Golden Corn Cakes with Crispy Pancetta and Arugula Salad, 70
- Herbed Chicken Paillards with Zucchini Pancakes and Cherry Tomato Pan Sauce, 138
- Lamb Kebabs with Harissa, Chickpeas, and Summer Squash, 111
- Pad Thai, 36
- Panko-Fried Crab Cakes with Heirloom Tomato, Nectarine, and Avocado Salad, 193
- Salade Niçoise, 200
- Scallops and Asian Noodle Salad with Spicy Lime Sauce, 198

ONE PAN, TWO PLATES

- Skirt Steak Fajitas with Pico de Gallo and Avocado, 90
- Stir-Fried Ginger Shrimp with Sugar Snap Peas, Red Bell Peppers, and Corn, 196
- Summer Rolls with Shrimp, Cucumber, and Mango, 38
- Tuna Burgers with Wasabi Mayo and Quick Cucumber Pickle, 61

falling leaves (autumn meals)

- Barley Risotto with Sweet Potato and Andouille Sausage, 42
- Black Cod Fillets Poached in Five-Spice Broth with Baby Bok Choy and Udon, 181
- Braised Chicken Thighs with Wild Rice, Walnuts, and Grapes, 152
- Braised Lentils with Polish Kielbasa and Cabbage, 68
- Cornflake-Crusted Chicken Fingers with Rosemary–Sweet Potato Pan Fries and Chutney Dipping Sauce, 135
- Crispy Sage Pork Cutlets with Couscous, Peas, Figs, and Pistachios, 76
- Croque Madame, 54
- Cuban Sandwiches, 56
- Flat-Iron Steak with Green Beans, Chili-Hoisin Sauce, and Sesame Seeds, 94
- Fresh Pepper Linguine with Olive Oil–Packed Tuna, Capers, and Golden Raisins, 28
- Herb-Rubbed Pork with Honey-Lime Roasted Sweet Potatoes, Cauliflower, and Major Grey's Chutney, 82
- Lo Mein Noodles with Chicken, Snow Peas, and Peanut Sauce, 34
- Mujaddara with Onions, Dried Apricots, Almonds, and Spicy Yogurt, 52
- Spicy Orange Beef Stir-Fry with Snow Peas and Carrots, 86
- Spinach-and-Cheese Tortellini with Leeks and Creamy Mushroom Sauce, 32
- Thai Red Curry Chicken with Bell Peppers and Broccoli, 150
- Thyme-Dusted Pork Medallions with Pear-Rutabaga Mash, 74
- Thyme-Rubbed Salmon with Shallots and Caramelized Cauliflower "Risotto," 166

- Turkey Tonkatsu with Cabbage, Portobellos, and Pickled Ginger, 126
- Veal Piccata with Brussels Sprout Hash and Apples, 104
- Veal Rolls with Currants, Pine Nuts, and Parmesan Polenta Stacks, 109
- Wild Mushroom Frittata with Cheddar, Green Onions, and Peas, 123

baby it's cold outside (winter meals)

- Balsamic-Braised Chicken Thighs with Figs and Creamy Polenta, 154
- Beef Stew in High Heels, 102
- Braised Lentils with Polish Kielbasa and Cabbage, 68
- Buffaloed Chicken Legs with Braised Celery and Roquefort Smashed Potatoes, 156
- Creamy Yukon Gold Potato Gratin with Ham, 72
- Flash-Roasted Tilapia with New Potatoes, Peas, and Pesto Mayonnaise, 176
- Fontina and Prosciutto–Stuffed Chicken Breasts with Radicchio-Fennel Sauté, 146
- Haddock with Shiitake Mushrooms and Black-Eyed Pea Ragù, 188
- Hungarian Beef Goulash with Paprika and Dumplings, 99
- Jambalaya with Chicken, Shrimp, and Andouille Sausage, 47
- Lamb Korma, 114
- One-Pan Roast Deviled Chicken with Carrots, Turnips, and Parsnips, 141
- Pasta Carbonara, 30
- Poached Halibut with Chive Gremolata, Brussels Sprouts, and Butter Bean Mash, 186
- Rib-Eye Steaks Florentine with Parsnip-and-Potato Galettes, 92
- Sautéed Chicken Breasts with Lemon and Winter Greens, 143
- Sweet-and-Sour Stir-Fry with Beef, Broccoli, and Mango, 88
- Three-Cheese Mac with Crispy Prosciutto, 19
- Turkey Chili with Poblano and Queso Fresco, 130

- Veal Rolls with Currants, Pine Nuts, and Parmesan Polenta Stacks, 109
- Winter Frittata with Escarole, Bacon, and Feta Cheese, 121

meatless mondays (vegetarian meals)

- Fluffy Spring Frittata with Asparagus, Bell Peppers, and Gruyère, 118
- Fresh Summer Pasta with Tomatoes, Garlic, Basil, and Buttery Croutons, 21
- Lemony Risotto with Asparagus, Carrots, and Chives, 45
- Mujaddara with Onions, Dried Apricots, Almonds, and Spicy Yogurt, 52
- Spinach-and-Cheese Tortellini with Leeks and Creamy Mushroom Sauce, 32
- Vegetable Biryani with Green Beans, Cauliflower, and Carrots, 50
- Wild Mushroom Frittata with Cheddar, Green Onions, and Peas, 123

easily adapted to vegetarian

- Barley Risotto with Sweet Potato and Andouille Sausage (or not), 42
- Braised Lentils with Polish Kielbasa (or not) and Cabbage, 68
- Creamy Yukon Gold Potato Gratin with Ham (or not), 72
- Croque Madame (omit the ham), 54
- Fried Green Tomato Sandwiches with Bacon (or not) and Chutney, 59
- Golden Corn Cakes with Crispy Pancetta (or not) and Arugula Salad, 70
- Lo Mein Noodles with Chicken (or not), Snow Peas, and Peanut Sauce, 34
- Pad Thai (leave out the shrimp), 36
- Salade Niçoise (omit the tuna), 200
- Summer Rolls with Shrimp (or not), Cucumber, and Mango, 38
- Three-Cheese Mac with Crispy Prosciutto (or not), 19

index

acknowledgments

I'd like to give thanks to my dad, Eugene Lewis Ferguson, who loved to tickle his taste buds. He unwittingly guided me into the culinary arts, first with the genetic gift of his palate and later with his 1970s *Gourmet* magazines, which kick-started my culinary life.

Thank you to the extraordinary people at Chronicle Books for creating the most beautiful cookbooks in the business. I send much gratitude to my editor, Bill LeBlond, for his vision of this book and the encouragement to write it my way; to editor Amy Treadwell for her expert eye and unerring advice; to managing editors Doug Ogan and Claire Fletcher for cleaning and polishing the manuscript till it sparkled; and to copyeditor Carrie Bradley Neves for her tireless attention to detail. *Mille mercis* to art director Alice Chau, designer Cat Grishaver, and photographer Jody Horton for creating a fun, easy-to-read yet beautiful book to be proud of for many years to come. Kudos to lead production coordinator Tera Killip, marketing manager Peter Perez, and publicity manager David Hawk for putting ink to paper and for packaging and promoting *One Pan, Two Plates* to the masses.

Thanks to my mentor, Zona Spray, for giving me the opportunity to work with the best and to learn and grow as a cook and teacher at the Zona Spray School of Cooking; and later to Carole Ferguson and the amazing staff of the Western Reserve School of Cooking.

Kisses and hugs to John McMillan and the Bun Babes at Great Lakes Baking Company. Baking delicious pastry and bread was never more fun.

With appreciation to my countless students and friends who've recipe tested and critiqued over the years: Julie Neri, Mary Lohman, Sarah McNally, Brigitte Gottfried, Anne Pitkin, Wendy Hilty, Tammy Karasek, Mary Kiefer, Terri Thompson, Sarina Kinney, Mary Anne Kickel, Maria Isabella, Ann Richardson, Karen Fish, Anne Gallagher, Elsa de Cardenas, Mary Sprunt, Mary Jones, Janet Redman, Auddie Gundling, Gayle Joyce, Bud Long, Mickey Shankland, Barb Synek, Kathy Belden, Beth Balzarini, Jamie Stevens, Sue Koob, Barb VanBlarcum, Rosie deQuattro, Laura Micco, John and Kim LaScola, Elaine George, and Bob and Theresa Delphus. I really, really couldn't do it without you.

Special thanks to my kids, Jessica, Justin, and Corey, and daughters-in-law, Lyndsey and Sara, for always lending a helpful hand at family dinners and get-togethers. Whether it's chopping vegetables, setting the table, or doing the dishes, I love spending time in the kitchen with you.

And last but not least, to my loving husband, Rick, who gave me the kitchen of my dreams and happily eats everything on his plate. Thanks for being hungry.